The Remarkable

Coach

The Remarkable Coach

Published by One Acorn Press in the United Kingdom 2024

Paperback ISBN: 978-2-9587000-0-3
Ebook ISBN: 978-2-9587000-1-0

Copyright © Karen Kissane, 2024

Images © Karen Kissane, 2024

Publishing partnership with The Writing House
www.thewritinghouse.co.uk

Cover design by Kieron Lewis
KieronLewis.com

Typesetting by The Book Typesetters
www.thebooktypesetters.com

The Remarkable Coach

The 9-Step Framework to Build a Thriving Coaching or Online Business

Karen Kissane

For Kris, who showed me how coaches can transform lives, including their own.

Introductions First

If there's one thing I'm sure of, it's that becoming a remarkable coach and growing a thriving business is possible for everyone. How do I know? Because I did it, and if you have the right strategy, confidence and attitude, you can too.

I started exactly where you are now: sat at the kitchen table, trying to work it all out. I did a happy dance over the first coaching package I sold. It was a 50% off deal – £300 for six sessions. I was a brand-new coach and sold it to my pro-bono training clients as a thank-you. Three said yes.

I remember sitting in the kitchen with my husband, thinking: if I could make my corporate salary of £75,000, I'd be quids in. I'd be home, spending more time with my children…

But I broke every rule.

I undervalued my time.

I charged by the session and hour. So, to make £75,000, I'd be working more hours than was humanly possible.

I didn't have a clear niche.

I wasn't sure how to get enough people to buy from me.

I had a scattergun approach and a to-do list a mile long.

And I said I could coach anyone with pretty much any business.

A few years down the line, it's a very different story that proves that when things take off, they can snowball. Now, consistently high revenue months are the norm. I have a team, and money isn't a worry. And for this, I am grateful.

I want to show you how to navigate your way from the kitchen table most of us start from, to owning the coaching business that gives you the freedom and income you have always dreamed of, but haven't yet made a reality.

I have worked with thousands of coaches, new and established. My mission is to help great coaches build great coaching businesses – because this is not a given. Often, I see amazing coaches not making money years after starting. They have bold ambitions, and try for months, years even, to get their business going, but are not moving forward as fast as they expected. During that time, the frustration grows, and their self-doubt is off the scale.

They often don't have enough predictable revenue to cover their outgoings or to leave their 9-5, causing massive financial worry. It breaks my heart because spending the best part of a year training and qualifying as a coach takes lots of dedication. People think the training is the hard part and the work is done. Except, it's the other way around. Building their business is where the true work, self-belief, determination, and perseverance are needed.

I've stood in the same shoes, wondering what everyone is doing that I'm not and why it's so hard to get clients. Without business experience in things like marketing, client attraction, messaging, and sales, it will be hard. Yet so many struggle but continue to insist on doing it alone.

The stakes are usually high. Often everything in a new coach's life rides on getting their business off the ground as it's been their plan for the last couple of years. But it's painfully slow because they don't know how to go about doing it.

This is where I want to help. Here, you'll learn my Signature Framework, which includes the nine essential elements of creating a highly profitable coaching business. These are the steps that will take you from where you are currently to where you want to be.

Most new coaches have had past careers, experiences, interests, or family lives shaping the kind of coach they want to be. It can define their niche and build trust with future clients – we might be new to coaching and building a business, but we all have a wealth of broader influences to draw on. So, why did I get into coaching? It's a story of how your worst day can turn out to be your best.

A few years before, I was a scientist. But back then, I was working as a researcher at Oxford University, where I spent my days inside the lab sequencing DNA and figuring out the answers to groundbreaking questions. After a few years, I noticed the reps coming in to demonstrate their state-of-the-art equipment. They'd do a presentation, take our samples and run them through formulas, generating results for us more quickly and efficiently than we were used to, and pitch us the machine. They ran their diaries, had more freedom than I'd ever seen in a job, were given a company car, travelled to new places, and every time they made a sale, they earned even more money.

I wanted their job.

So, I took my research knowledge and my understanding of running experiments and stepped over into this new direction. Little did I know that this path would lead me to coaching.

I now had a well-paid job in a billion-dollar life sciences company with perks galore. It was freeing to plan my own diary. I was barely accountable to anyone except myself. What's more, I developed a solid determination to succeed by consistently hitting my sales targets and seeing the rewards. My sales job made me realise two things: I loved having a freed-up lifestyle, and I was motivated to hit numbers and targets.

Having done well in my sales job with the company I worked for, I was given the role of sales trainer. People invited me to train other teams and new starters. It couldn't have been a better next step. I revelled in this dual responsibility within the company – being in sales and training people.

I loved my job. I was good at it, did well, and never imagined leaving. That was until I returned to it from a nine-month maternity leave after I had my son. What greeted me wasn't what I had expected. I was told the person who'd taken over as the sales trainer in my absence would be keeping the role. I wouldn't get it back because, apparently, having a baby meant I couldn't fulfil my company responsibilities in the same way. I was crushed.

I couldn't believe what was happening. I had to endure an awful work environment until I finally decided to seek help from an employment law solicitor. It came to a point where I was ready to take the company to a tribunal. In the end, they paid me hush money to go quietly. The experience made me feel undervalued and betrayed. The stress, especially with having a baby, was exhausting. I had lost my identity in a double dose. Suddenly, I was a newly jobless (literally, not figuratively) mum. It was tough.

But it made me vow I'd never work for anyone else again. And this, my friend, was a pivotal moment. I had sworn to create my own success instead of someone else's. I wanted to run my own business.

This is exactly when my worst day turned out to be my best.

Leaving the job I had loved was tough. It hurt. But I came out of it with a newfound motivation to do things differently. The idea of becoming a business coach was something I hadn't planned on doing right after leaving my job. But as luck had it, things began falling into place.

Within days, people were asking me to do sales training within their companies. Before I knew it, I was invited into these offices to help companies improve their sales and marketing. It was an immense period of growth. With the wheels turning for my budding business as an independent sales trainer, I hatched my master plan.

I took the experience, knowledge, skills, determination, and ambition that I had and packaged it into something I could sell to companies. I spent a few years doing sales training, then realised I knew a lot about marketing too. I'd help companies attract leads and sell to them. Slowly, my services morphed into a strategic business development for entrepreneurs and small businesses. I found myself sitting with small businesses, making recommendations on how to grow and guiding them on how to make more money.

At that time, I was advising and consulting. But I soon realised the power of a different approach. I asked questions, and these brought in different answers. Asking powerful questions made my clients more motivated and likely to take action. They were empowering themselves to drive their own business forward and generate results. Without realising it, I had discovered coaching. This combination of mentoring and coaching is, for my clients and for me, a change-making approach.

Understandably, I wanted to be the best coach I could possibly be. I knew the more I improved, the better I could help clients with their businesses. So, I learned and immersed myself in everything related to coaching. I set aside enough time and resources to acquire training to go alongside my sales and marketing expertise, as well as complement my practice in consultancy and business development. I gained qualifications in coaching, with top grades, and became a coach mentor for the organisation I trained with.

Armed with this training, I married my coaching skills with business. And I've been developing ever since. Learning, doing the work, and being brave enough to take risks was a truly life-changing experience. Achieving the success I have now would not have been possible if I hadn't chosen to invest in myself and my skills. This is something I want to highlight to you throughout this book. If you want to move forward and do great things with your business, you must be willing to invest in your development. And have the courage to go for it.

But becoming a qualified coach was just the beginning. I decided I wanted to make an impact and work with as many people as I could. So, I took to the internet and steadily built an online presence. The more people I was able to reach, the more my business grew. So, in 2018, I took a leap of faith and launched The Smart Woman brand and The Smart Woman's Business Hub community. It was my way of bringing together this online community I had started for women so they could accelerate the growth of their businesses. The group later rebranded as Remarkable, the hangout for remarkable coaches, consultants, and course creators as my niche became more refined and I began to work with more and more men.

When I look back at everything that has happened, one of the most pivotal moments that shaped my coaching journey might not be what you would expect – it involved a relocation to France.

Moving to France was one of the things that required me to be braver than ever before. It started with my husband's previous job. He was a partner in a business, but over time, he became disillusioned and stressed out. It wasn't a fun time for him or us. We decided that the best thing for him to do would be to quit his job.

This was a huge decision. He was going to leave the high-paying job he'd been in for fifteen years. That meant it was up to me and my business to see us through. I needed to step things up to support him and our two children. So, we set our plan. My husband would leave his job, we would sell our UK home, move to France, buy a property that could generate some income, and I would run my business from there.

We wanted to seize life and make the most of it. We wanted to do something different. We wanted change. We were in a rut, and my husband's tough patch had made us realise life was passing us by. Most people spend their entire lives dreaming of something different but never going after it. We did just that and haven't looked back.

There's a caveat, though: it was hard work.

There were times I felt like we had bitten off more than we could chew. A new country, a language to learn, kids to get settled, building projects, a business that had to grow, and the pressure of all of the family expenses firmly resting on my shoulders. There was no Plan B, so we had to make it work.

My business was doing okay before, but this move created an urgency that fuelled even more growth. We bought a chateau with event spaces, carried out a load of renovations, and we're now using it as an additional revenue stream for high-end holiday rentals and events. This is where I now hold luxury retreats and face-to-face events to support my business.

Fast forward three years, and here I am, with two children I am blessed to spend so much time with and a business that generates orders of magnitude more than my corporate salary ever did.

I have another business now as well, founded by myself and my incredible husband Ivan. Together we created CoachSpace.ai, a cutting-edge tech platform designed to help coaches build their business with more ease, speed and profit by automating the processes coaches need to build thriving businesses, including funnels, courses, list building, tracking opportunities, invoices, and more.

I have full autonomy over my day, the ability to be as creative as I like, and the potential for exponential growth. I'm my own boss, and I'm at home making choices and can take a holiday whenever I want. There's no daily commute, and I can plan my day and do whatever I wish. I'm creating my own wealth, not someone else's.

My worst day definitely turned out to be my best.

In most situations in our everyday life, we don't have this kind of urgency (such as suddenly moving to a different country and becoming the family's sole breadwinner). We tend to let days go by without believing the time is now. We tell ourselves there's always another day, only to realise later that months have passed, and our business is still nowhere near where we want it to be.

So, here is my first question for you:

How can you create your own urgency?

Growing a business requires enormous perseverance, belief, and a strategy to get you in front of the right people so they see what they will get from working with you.

There's a lot to think about. It's not about posting on social media a few times a week and hoping the clients will come. There are many things to consider and optimise. People don't know what they don't know and will miss the crucial steps that make the biggest difference.

My mission is to help my clients massively reduce the time it takes to make all of this happen. Because otherwise, it can easily take a year, or longer. Some might never get there, or they might charge so little out of frustration, attract the wrong people, and end up with an expensive hobby that doesn't pay the bills. Or end up having to return to their 9-5 and let go of the dream of their own business.

In *The Remarkable Coach*, I'll guide you on how to shorten the time it takes to build a remarkable coaching business by taking the right steps at the right moment. Trial and error can take decades. And this might be time you can't afford to lose. Let's begin this journey of seismic shifts by first considering the kind of coach you really want to be.

The Kind of Coach You *Really* Want to Be

All you have to do is open Instagram and see polished images of coaches jet-setting around the world and sipping cocktails by the pool to feel like a fish out of water when it comes to starting your coaching business. Let's call our bikini-clad coach on Instagram, Kate.

We all know that living the laptop lifestyle in Bali, working only two hours a day and jet-setting to different places doesn't completely depict what being a coach is like. Whether Kate's business is successful or not, this image paints a picture of freedom, wealth, and opportunity. And while we all aspire to have freedom like this, for most of us the reality is different, especially at the start. As new coaches, we look at our list of tasks and zero clients and see a vast expanse between ourselves and other coaches.

On the other side of the spectrum to Kate is the second type of coach. She goes by the name of Emily. She is an amazing coach. She's done the hard work to get her coach training qualifications. She knows her stuff and is willing to put in her 100% to help clients. But unlike Kate, whose business is thriving, Emily is struggling to get hers off the ground.

She's basically a great coach, without a great coaching business.

Her business is playing small, even though she is incredibly talented. What's more, seeing successful, Instagram-famous coaches like Kate makes Emily feel inadequate even though she's possibly more qualified as a coach and is just as able to create an impact in her clients' lives.

But despite their differences, Kate and Emily faced similar challenges when building a coaching business they can be proud of and that gives them the life they want.

Now, let's talk for a minute about these two coaches' mindsets. Because the way they think about their business has the ability to make or break things. And it's the same for you.

Your thoughts, beliefs, attitudes, ideas, and the limitations you place on yourself, either consciously or subconsciously, determine the type of business you end up with and your degree of success. This underpins everything. Overthinking, fear and perfectionism are real challenges that stop great coaches from cultivating remarkable coaching businesses.

What's more, from my experience working with thousands of coaches and building my own high revenue coaching business, most coaches just don't know *how*.

How to get going.

How to get their first clients.

How to create momentum.

And how to reach those high-revenue months everyone online is talking about.

Most coaches don't have a background in business, yet they set out on this learning journey with earning aspirations that far exceed their corporate careers. These are the same careers they spent decades developing, yet with the click of a finger, they expect the same, if not more, money flowing into their bank accounts each month.

Despite this (and there's nothing wrong with wanting to make vast sums of money), they waste months, even years, figuring things out without results. They don't know what they don't know.

A few years down the line, many consider throwing the towel in as they've been unable to make it work or resign themselves to making 'pocket money' because they haven't been able to figure out the secret sauce to blowing things up.

This is what I want you to know:

It's not that hard to build a remarkable coaching business – when you know how.

Trying to figure it out on your own is the fastest way to frustration.

Trial and error will take years – decades, even. It's like building a house by yourself, without any knowledge of how foundations work or even how to use a trowel. As a result, you'll end up with a substandard house or no house at all.

That's why you need to understand that your biggest limitation is that 'you don't know what you don't know.' The key to this lies with your mindset and letting go of the need to struggle, figure stuff out on your own or bootstrap your coaching business.

Overthinking, perfectionism, putting things off for another day, undercharging, hiding in the shadows, playing small, and unnecessary faffing with the copy on page seven of your website instead of having conversations with potential clients, all of these limit how well you do as a coach. It comes down to your mindset.

To show you how mindset can limit your coaching business, let me tell you about one of my clients when she started working with me. Laura is a copywriter and coach who helps female entrepreneurs create copy and content that attracts their dream clients. She's talented at what she does and one of the best copywriters I've come across, but her mindset was holding her back from achieving the levels of success she was capable of.

She didn't have the confidence, at first, to post her own content and put herself out there. Her fear of being visible on social media, combined with her perfectionism, put the brakes on her business growth. It was by confronting this and showing up for herself that Laura turned things around. Now, she has a thriving business and is doing amazing work as a copywriter and coach. Ultimately, Laura was able to unlock her potential, create a remarkable impact for her clients, and build a business she's proud of.

And it is this third type of coach that many strive to be.

The coach who creates the results they want

Laura is now the kind of coach who will go all in.

She can confidently bet on herself. And she does this by combining the right energy and motivation with a powerful business-building strategy. She understands that how you show up is everything to do with the success you create.

And I don't just mean now and then. I mean consistently. The person you are, the perseverance to keep going, and the passion you have for your work. You can be this kind of coach. You can choose to be courageous and capable of creating unstoppable success with these three things:

1. The Right Strategy

Posting on social media and hoping for clients is not a strategy. Offering your services to just about anyone who expresses interest in working with you is not a strategy. But I see a lot of coaches and consultants doing this.

As a result, they blend into the background. They have a generic brand that looks the same as everyone else's. And I don't want that for you. Which is why you need a proper strategy and plan. What are you aiming for? What is working? Where are the gaps? What do you need to give your attention to? This is what will make the difference between you never scoring versus achieving everything you want *and more*.

2. The Confidence to Take Action

Confidence is essential. You can have the best strategy but if you don't have the confidence to support that, then implementation becomes really challenging.

Bravery, courage, grit. Call it what you will. It's all the same thing. The point is you need to be confident to take inspired action and follow your strategy. Without that, you won't achieve your potential.

In business, the hard part isn't always knowing what to do. The hard part is doing it. And this is where confidence makes the most impact. Because one of the telltale signs of a lack of confidence is procrastination. Most people don't do the things they want to do. Not because they can't. Not because they're not smart enough. But because they don't know how, and put it off for another day. You might hear yourself making excuses like these instead of embracing the confidence to act:

"I'm too busy today."

"The kids are at home."

"There's a lot on my plate."

"I'll just finish my website first…" (And months later you're still changing the font size.)

Discard these statements. Remember, confidence leads to action, and action to success. Confidence is the difference between thinking about doing something and doing it.

3. An Attitude to Succeed No Matter What

This is the most essential aspect of becoming a remarkable coach.

I could give you the process and the strategy right now. We could map this out, and you could be my client. We could do all of that. But the mindset you have – including how you show up and the energy you have for your business – is what will ultimately help you create the success you want.

All your decisions and choices can significantly change the course of your business. If you have a mindset that is holding you back, you probably won't make the key decisions needed to grow your business. So, look closely at your mindset. Is it helping you? Or is it stopping you from growing?

This is a lot to do with being a 'yes' person with the curiosity to discover and try things without the fear of the unknown or getting it wrong.

To reach a different outcome, you need a different kind of coach

In the next chapter, I'll walk you through an overview of my nine-step Signature Framework. This plan encapsulates the principles I use to bring about the three key elements above, and you won't find these with any other coach.

Because a different kind of coaching framework requires a different kind of coach. Here are some of the things that are unique to my approach:

- I think like a scientist because I am a scientist

  My background as a molecular biologist means I work to solve problems quickly and efficiently. My logical, practical, and solution-based methods create momentum and results. I apply this thinking every day in my own business. My clients will tell you that I often say running a business is like running an experiment as we don't always know how things will work out. We don't know the combinations of buttons to press to get the desired results so we must test, tweak, refine and adjust. I learn, I refine, and I evolve. This legacy, carried over from being a scientist, serves me very well today.

- I don't make promises I can't keep

  You will never hear me say I will help you make six figures in your business by next weekend. Or that there's a magic blueprint with guaranteed results. This is down to you. Your motivation and will to succeed, your work ethic, mindset, the knowledge you have and how you apply it, your level of risk, and the time you have all contribute to your success.

  I can give you all the tools you need, but you must do the work.

- I hate the word 'hustle'

  I help coaches and service-based businesses have extraordinary lives by building a remarkable business that's simple and powerful. I'm not about the hustle. I'm not about the eighteen-hour days. My signature approach is an anti-hustle 'less is more' one where we scale simply. Of course, you need to work hard to move your business forward, and there will be some long days ahead. But I also want you to have an amazing life that goes alongside that business. Having a lucrative business at the expense of your life is just not worth it.

  And that's why I'm a life coach AND a business coach. Because these things go hand in hand.

- I prioritise simplicity over complexity

  I'm a big advocate of keeping things simple. Approaching your business with simplicity is how you grow and scale. I've learnt the hard way, believe me.

  People overcomplicate things all the time. Too many ideas, garbled messaging, fancy funnels that don't work, and a zillion haphazard offers. It's exhausting with dozens of things going on.

  We need less, not more.

So, if you're ready to take action and become the coach who can bet on yourself, and if you're going all in to achieve that, this book will show you how. You'll learn about the nine steps of my Signature Framework that not only made my coaching business catapult to levels I never thought possible but have been proven to work repeatedly by hundreds of my clients' businesses. What often separates a great coach from a great coaching business is a mindset gap or a skills gap. I am here to help you determine which applies to you in each area of your business and provide the solutions to both.

In the next chapter, I'll show you the pieces of the online coaching business puzzle that, when they come together, create the recipe for a remarkable coach.

Key Points:

- Your thoughts, beliefs, attitudes, ideas, and the limitations you place on yourself, consciously or subconsciously, determine your type of business and overall success.
- Having the right strategy is only part of the puzzle and this needs to be combined with the confidence to take action and an attitude to succeed no matter what.

Introducing the Signature Framework

B eing a great coach is not the same as having a great coaching business. I realised this pretty quickly when I began working with my first clients. So, how do you transform yourself into a remarkable coach with a thriving business? It's not that hard to get your coaching business up and running, when you think about it…

There are no products to buy.

There's no stock or premises needed.

There are very few overheads.

The costs to get going are low. All you really need is a decent internet connection and the ability to translate your skills, knowledge, and experience into something that helps people – and that they're willing to pay for.

Easy right?

So why do so many new coaches find it agonisingly slow to build momentum and earn a decent living? This is why:

There are steps to follow that many people miss. They focus on the wrong things and get lost down a rabbit hole of confusion, ultimately overwhelmed by their lack of progress. This means they begin to doubt themselves, wondering if they'll ever 'make it', and constantly feeling the financial pinch. The nine steps of my Signature Framework will cover all the parts of starting out you may have missed, some of which you may have never thought about. Until all nine are in place, you'll be missing at least one key element that will give you the thriving business you are proud of and the time to enjoy your life.

The way I see it, coaches typically fall into three stages of growth, and may never move out of stage one or two if they don't make changes to their mindset or business model.

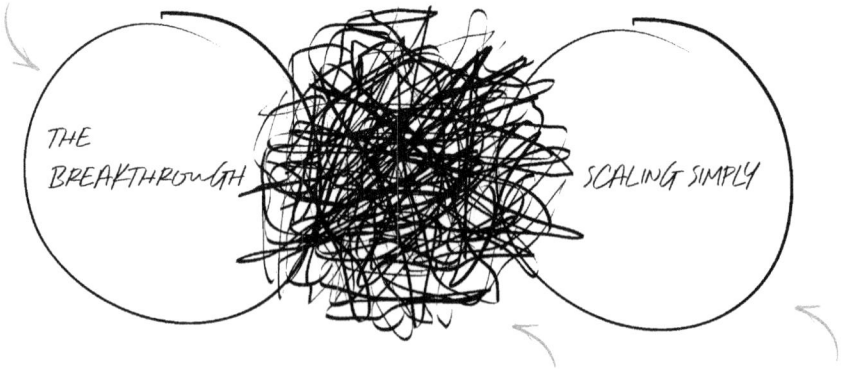

Stage one, 'The Breakthrough', is when you're starting and are likely to be *time-rich but client-poor*. You might have all the time in the world (unless you're building your coaching business alongside your job), and you spend most of that jumping around from one thing to the next. You're unsure what steps to take and what to work on.

Then at stage two, the tables turn, and as your diary fills, you become *client-rich but time-poor*. As you take in those clients and really build your business, you get busy. Most of your time is given to client delivery. While this is good, you don't have the capacity to develop your business or live your life. This is the 'Messy Middle'.

So, your goal is to reach stage three: being *client-rich and time-rich*. You have clients, you're making money in your business, and you have time as well. You can freely do the things you want and your business is 'Scaling Simply'.

How to achieve this is what this chapter will discuss – the nine-step Signature Framework to becoming a Remarkable Coach. Why are there nine? Here's the reality. You need to focus on multiple things within your business to get the results you want. Building a profitable coaching business means many moving parts – not just about one or two things.

Instead, it involves a suitcase of ideas, projects, and systems that should constantly be on your radar. When some of these are overlooked or if there are missing ingredients, you'll notice gaping holes that impact your results. There are certain levers that every coach needs to focus on and master.

Get More Leads
Get More Customers
Make More Money Per Sale
Make More Money Per Customer
Make More Profit
Build More Impact
Master Client Retention

Save More Time

Experience More Joy

It is these elements that informed my Signature Framework, which takes these outcomes and shows you *how* to achieve them.

If you aim for consistent progress in all the key areas I'll outline in this book, there's a good chance you'll build an incredible coaching business. You don't have to do things perfectly all the time. But you do have to be consistent in the work you put in. Small steps lead to big steps. When people attempt to make giant leaps, especially in a short time, that's when things fall over because it's unsustainable. And exhausting.

You'll be surprised how quickly things can snowball with clients and money flowing in. You just need to know the right steps to take and in which order to make it happen.

So, let's begin with a quick overview of the Signature Framework so you know the areas you will focus on. Then, in the following chapters, we will take a deep dive into each one so that you have all the tools to put the strategies in place.

1. Set yourself up for success

Setting yourself up for success is about the daily habits and routines you bring into your life to support the growth of your business.

We can all picture the business we aspire to have. But how far from that picture are you, and what are the steps you need to get closer? Success doesn't happen overnight. We don't click our fingers and have it all right in front of us on a golden platter. We make changes and improvements slowly, starting with how we live. We must set ourselves up for success and bring into our life the elements that support where we are heading.

The small things add up to the big things. Often people skip the fundamentals, and that's what this step is all about – ensuring you're setting yourself up for success from the outset. Because if you don't, you'll end up frustrated, overwhelmed, and struggling, and ultimately feel like it's just not working. First, it is an intention, then a behaviour, then a habit, then a practice, then second nature, before it is simply who you are.

To set yourself up for success, there are six parts you will go through:

- Your Mindset Matters

     Change and success start with how you think. Your mindset plays a central role in your ability to take action and how you handle difficult situations. Without a strong mindset, you might talk yourself out of something instead of just doing it. Or maybe start something but don't finish it because you're unclear on the next steps. To reach success, the first and most important action is to develop the right mindset to help you move forward instead of stopping you from achieving your goals.

- Your Success Habits

  Success comes from taking steady, intelligent action every single day. It doesn't have to be groundbreaking, but it does have to be consistent, from your daily habits to your decisions. Such action involves adjusting your daily routine and practices to bring you closer to success.

- Your Business Today

  This action is about doing an audit of your business. By audit, I mean assessing your current reality and conducting a review to ascertain where the gaps are, where your strengths lie and what your key focus areas should be.

- Your Roadmap

  Your roadmap is your plan for success. In this action, you identify your goals and create the strategy that will lead you to them.

- Your Financial Targets

  The best way to achieve your goals is to break them down into stepping stones – this applies to your financial targets, too. If you want to hit a certain monthly profit goal, what products and services can you sell to reach this figure?

- Embracing your Queen Bee Role
  As the owner of your coaching business, embrace your leadership role. This means delegating tasks that others within your business can complete and using your precious time to focus on what only you can do.

2. Know the pillars of your business

There's no point trying to run before you can walk. To do this you must ensure the foundations of your business are in place. And if it has stalled, is stuck, or you've hit a plateau, returning to your pillars will help you to get back to basics and on track.

Your business pillars encompass your brand, story, and message – you want to make sure they shine through everything you do, creating a consistent identity for your business. Every business needs an identity. What makes you unique, and why should people buy from you rather than your competitors?

Your business needs direction and a foundation. It needs coherence and a compass for your leadership. When you know what your business stands for, having defined these business pillars, you'll know how and what to communicate.

Your brand identity is the personality of your business. It's the story underpinning your message (how you communicate what you do and why people should work with you) and your pillars (the building blocks of your business). What principles or ideas make up your brand?

It's easy to mimic and replicate what other people are doing, especially when you're starting out. It's hard to find your voice at the beginning, and it seems faster and easier to piggyback off what someone else is doing. But it's important that you don't do that. Because you're not them, and they're not you. It'll be awkward and inauthentic. You have to find your own way and, after a while, people start to identify your words with you. Connections are formed. Credibility is built.

If you're repeatedly talking about the same things, particularly things that make your business unique, that's what you will become known for. When you talk about anything and everything or jump from one thing to the next, it dilutes your message. It lessens the potential power of your business and weakens your individuality.

3. Understanding your product or service and the problem it solves

The third step involves getting clear on your products or services and the specific problems they solve. To do this, you must know what people need and how you can provide the solution they're looking for.

Ask yourself what is the problem that they need to be fixed. What's the best solution? And how can you be the person to provide it? When you're clear on that, the process of identifying your message becomes a whole lot easier.

This is about you helping *who* to achieve *what* by *how*. It's about the outcomes, transformations, and benefits people will get from working with you.

No matter your business, products and services, you need to know how you can help people. Otherwise, you can't get clear on your messaging and won't attract people to your business. This doesn't mean just listing all the features of what you sell. Instead, it's about clarifying what that feature means to the person buying it. What value and benefit does it give your potential client? And what is your best method of delivery?

If you already have great services or products, know how they can help people, communicate your brand pillars, and set your goals, then all you need is to package all of that into something people actually want to buy.

4. Create irresistible offers

Having more than one revenue stream in your business makes a lot of sense. When I look at what I've done in my business over the last few years, I've created multiple ways to make money, help people, and deliver my coaching. If I were just doing one type of thing all the time, I'd get bored. I love the diversity of projects I take on. It keeps me engaged and interested.

But importantly, it enables people to jump into my coaching at different price points depending on what my prospects and clients need. One of the biggest lessons for me when I started as a coach was meeting people where they are at. If you're a coach and only offering one way clients can work with you, what happens when a potential client likes you but doesn't like your offer? Well, you risk losing that prospect simply because you have nothing else to sell to them. It won't really matter if they like you and are interested in your business.

So, it's a good idea in terms of your business model to generate multiple revenue streams at different price points. Create different ways people can work with you. Meet them where they are at and step them through your programmes as they grow and continue working with you. It's not where they start – it's where they end up that matters.

You don't need to do all of this from the beginning if you're still in the early stages of your business. But it's something you should map out as your business grows.

5. Building Consistent, Predictable Revenue

One of the biggest killers in any business is unpredictable revenue. You might have clients coming into your business, but you can't say with certainty when this will happen. This will leave you with high-income months and months where you hardly earn anything. You won't be able to plan or forecast, and this will mean your business plateaus.

The way to change this is by introducing a clear sales funnel. This is the customer journey from when they become aware of you, your services or product, all the way through to becoming a customer. Sales funnels can be as simple or complex as you want, and you can have multiple sales funnels or just one.

6. Build more visibility

If a tree falls in the forest and no one is around to hear it, does it make a sound? Your visibility and how to market yourself are the next step in creating success. If you're running an incredible coaching business, but no one knows you exist, how will you help those who really need you? Your visibility and getting noticed are key.

The people who need you, need to know you're there. You've started your business to help people, right? Generally, coaches are led by their hearts and want to do good in the world. But if you're not being seen, you're not able to help people.

Often, people's own sense of self – their ego – is what stops them. They are worried about what people will think, how they look or sound, whether they are professional enough, etc.

The good news is, it's not about you. When you stop making it about you and make it about your ideal clients instead, being visible feels amazing.

7. Craft a winning content strategy

Social media is such a powerful tool for coaches and business owners. You and I are extremely fortunate to be running businesses in this age. We have free platforms to share our work and grow our audience through making connections and building relationships.

Social media allows us to connect with and have conversations with so many people. Your potential clients are out there, just waiting to connect with someone who can help them to change, improve or achieve. Decades ago, this wouldn't have been possible in terms of numbers and ease.

The alternative then was putting flyers through letter boxes or placing an advert in magazines and newspapers. Social media has transformed the landscape of running a business and creating impact and influence.

So, it makes sense to embrace social media. Pick the channels and platforms that are right for you and your business. You can strategise where you want to grow your audience and build marketing campaigns accordingly. Leverage the technology at your fingertips. Because so many people want to hear from you right now, and these channels are your routes straight to them.

8. Sell confidently

The next thing you need is to learn how to sell confidently. And enjoy it!

Too many coaches are hesitant to sell. A good way to shift your thinking on this is to view it not as selling but as a way of supporting people. It's your way of connecting and serving clients to get to where they want to go. They might not get there otherwise. Don't think of it as just making a sale. The money you receive is the byproduct of doing the work you love and helping people.

You need to be okay with having conversations about money. You need to get comfortable saying, "Well, this is how much it costs. And this is the time I'm putting into this, and this is how it will help you." If you're afraid to have those conversations, you'll keep yourself small. You'll leave money on the table and, importantly, deny people the chance to change their lives by working with you.

But if you learn to enjoy the process of serving your clients and do it confidently, you'll have a huge impact and the revenue that comes with this.

9. Implement systems so your business runs like clockwork

They say a business is only as solid as the systems that support it. When you're doing all the heavy lifting yourself, things will fall between the cracks, opportunities will be missed, and your business might feel clunky and chaotic. You may also not have reliable ways to measure your results and effectiveness.

By support systems, I'm talking about the tech that makes

your life easier and the people who can help you. I felt so passionately about this I created my own tech platform to support coaches, CoachSpace.ai. Needing to have a strategy, understanding your messaging, and creating offers are all important, but what makes the difference to coaches is being able to automate, systemise and streamline their activities. That's why I created CoachSpace.ai with my business mentor and my husband. The three of us built the perfect platform for coaches to run their entire businesses from, freeing them to focus on their clients and business opportunities.

So many of us, myself included, start this entrepreneurial journey thinking we can do it all. You might think you don't need help right now because your business is still in its early stages. Or you're not in a position financially to ask for help. But somewhere down the line, you need to accept that you don't have to do everything. As your business grows, it's vital to have the right people around you so you can focus on your genius zone and minimise becoming overwhelmed. Yes, it's possible to do it all, but only up to a point. If you want to reach high revenue months and build a multi-dimensional business, you're going to have to let other people support you. Those people include outsourced freelancers, coaches and mentors who will guide you in catapulting your business to the next level.

By following these nine steps, you can make so many great and positive changes in your coaching business. This is why we'll spend the next chapters discussing them in much more detail, starting with how to set yourself up for success.

KEY POINTS

- Being a great coach is not the same as having a great coaching business.
- Coaches typically fall into one of three stages of growth: being time-rich but client-poor, being client-rich but time-poor or being client-rich and time-rich.
- The Signature Framework I'm going to share with you will show you how to move from the first two stages into being client-rich and time-rich.

Step #1:

Setting Yourself Up for Success

Setting yourself up for success is about the daily habits and routines you bring into your life to support the growth of your business. Success doesn't happen overnight, but the small things add up to the big ones. First, it is an intention, then a behaviour, then a habit, then a practice, then second nature. Finally, it is simply who you are.

1

Setting Yourself Up for Success

The very first step you must take to grow your coaching business is to set yourself up for success. It is the foundation that can't be skipped, or you'll quickly run up against limitations or head off in the wrong direction. Step One of the Signature Framework is about having a crystal-clear understanding of what you want to achieve and why.

We know that goal setting is an important part of any achievement. It's crucial because without knowing where you are heading, how can you hope to get there? And if you don't know where that is, we'll figure this out together in this chapter.

In this important first step, you'll pull together your plan, mindset and success habits and gain clarity on what comes next. The process I am about to share is the one I take all my clients through who I work with one-to-one, particularly if they are about to launch a coaching business or already have launched and are overwhelmed. This is a common theme amongst coaches in their first years of business. When I first spoke to my client, Ava, she was stressed, and so swamped with everything on her plate she ended up doing nothing.

1

Her marketing had basically stopped. She wasn't visible anywhere, and the leads were non-existent or had dried up altogether. She knew this was bad but couldn't see the wood for the trees. Ava felt she was going backwards in her coaching business and it was making her feel awful. So, to help fix this situation, I guided Ava to work through and identify her absolute priority. We removed other distractions and set a clear timeframe so she could focus on developing a roadmap for her business and set herself up for success. While going through this crucial first stage, she could double-down on her marketing because she knew the outcome she wanted.

Days after implementing this, Ava went from being paralysed by the volume of work on her plate to getting her head in the right place and quickly generating six new opportunities for her premium programme. Ava was no longer overwhelmed, and all it took to get her going again was to pause, craft a clear and detailed plan, and change her strategy.

More importantly, Ava let go of her negative mindset and replaced it with a proactive one. She learned to consistently practice the right mindset to get the results she wanted. This is how she was able to set herself up for success.

Like Ava, this is something you can accomplish, and together we will dive deeper into how you should go about it.

The 6 Actions to Setting Yourself Up for Success

1

Whatever success looks like to you, it's not usually something you'll achieve overnight. Success comes when everything works like clockwork in your business, and you have the systems and processes that ease the workload and do the heavy lifting. Something like this doesn't happen by accident, and it needs time to be put in place. It's a marathon not a sprint.

Whether you want to get more clients, improve your marketing, or simply be more organised, you will need to consistently put in the work and take intentional actions to increase your potential to succeed.

The small things that you do add up to the big things. And over time, you will see a shift in effectiveness.

When you take the time to set yourself up for success, you'll feel more prepared and motivated to work on your business. You'll know what your priorities are and why. You'll understand what might stop you and how to sail past the barriers that will undoubtedly appear.

There are six specific actions you can take to achieve success in your coaching business – whatever success may look like for you – and these begin with your mindset.

Action 1: Get in the right mindset

1

Your mindset plays a huge role in the outcomes you achieve. When you allow your mind to focus on negative feelings like being overwhelmed or discouraged, your actions will follow a similar path, leading to equally negative results.

On the other hand, maintaining a consistently healthy and positive mindset will help you see things clearly. Not only will you be able to confidently make decisions that will benefit your business, but you will also have a constant source of encouragement and determination.

Putting yourself in the right frame of mind, powerfully and energetically, is the first action in setting yourself up for success.

If you're in the right mindset, you'll achieve the things you set out for your business. You'll be able to clear the path and approach any challenge or task confidently. More importantly, all your thoughts and actions every day will motivate and inspire you.

The right mindset can teach you to see obstacles as learning experiences that will help you grow even further. With this, you will accept change and recover from failures more easily. You'll even be less afraid to take the risks you might not have thought possible. This is a key ingredient in allowing yourself to feel more empowered in your business because we all need to take risks to expand, and we will all occasionally experience failures when we take risks.

But when you stay in a limiting mindset, you will continue to doubt yourself. You'll allow your insecurities to get the better of you. As a result, you might talk yourself out of something instead of just doing it. Or focus on the easy things instead of activities that will make the biggest difference to your bottom line.

These decisions and choices will change the course of your business. You can either choose to dwell on your limitations and weaknesses or learn to recognise them and find solutions that propel you forward.

Getting into the right mindset means raising your self-awareness around your fears and challenges. Because when you don't identify them or make them visible, they'll remain buried, and you'll continue to wonder what is stopping you. Simply put, you can't fix something if you don't know what needs work.

So, Action 1 of setting yourself up for success is taking a good hard look at your mindset. Is it helping you? Or is it what's stopping you achieving your goals? And what can you change about your mindset right now that will put you on the right track?

To help you with this, below are five ways to build a stronger mindset:

1. Surround yourself with like-minded people
It's important to be aware of the types of people who make you feel the most safe, inspired, and confident. These are who you should spend the most time with. Think about who makes your life joyful and inspires you to be the greatest version of yourself. It could be your family, close friends, or the community you have built through your business.

1 Everyone's criteria for who they consider like-minded is different. But when it comes to business, you should surround yourself with people who are confident about being a CEO and continuously doing their best to improve themselves and their outcomes. When you have a network with whom you truly connect and can empathise with, you'll experience a wealth of advantages, which include:

- feeling secure being who you are
- expressing yourself honestly without worrying about your views, dreams, or issues being judged or misunderstood
- finding inspiration and motivation from others

2. Realise that comparison is the thief of joy

I won't say it's easy to avoid comparing yourself to others. The majority of us are accustomed to evaluating ourselves against other people. But I see too many coaches falling into the trap of becoming fixated with what other coaches are doing, which means less time focusing on what *they* are doing. They see coaches with more successful businesses, and feel demoralised because they haven't achieved the same.

But there comes a moment in life when comparing yourself to others does not serve you anymore. Comparisons are only constructive when they provide an idea of what you should aspire to and work towards. If you want to accomplish your finest work and fully express your unique skills as a coach and business owner, you must focus on what you are doing and try not to be distracted by what others are doing.

Their path is theirs, and you're on your own journey.

3. Try to see the good in every situation

Your perspective on life and business will have a big impact on how you react to challenging circumstances. But you always have the choice of how you will respond to the things that happen to you. You can choose to react negatively, or choose to seek the positives. You can remain anxious and stressed all the time or analyse the situation and devise a strategy. Even if we might not immediately notice it, a lesson is always waiting to be discovered.

4. Be willing to learn and change

The lessons we learn often require us to change our approach to similar situations in the future. Change can be good, especially when it involves changing your perspective, approach and limiting beliefs. The willingness to change, however, doesn't come as easily. You can say that you want to change and improve, but it won't amount to anything if you aren't willing to learn and adjust. If you want to make the kind of meaningful, long-lasting change you're after, you must act intentionally and purposefully.

5. Show gratitude

It's essential to recognise the things you're thankful for, both in your life and business. Expressing gratitude can help you engage more in what makes you happy and motivated. This also helps amplify your positive experiences because you focus more on them. You can change how you view yourself once you appreciate other people's contributions to your life and realise they value you.

Gratitude also stops you from comparing yourself to others and letting envy get the better of you. This is because envy and gratitude are incompatible. When you're grateful for what you have and accomplished, you can't resent someone else for having something you don't.

Action 2: Adjust your daily habits

What you choose to do with your time can either speed up or slow down your progress. The small habits you form in everyday life can ultimately lead to big changes for your business.

The most successful coaches didn't achieve success right away. Instead, they used their time productively so their business could prosper without sacrificing the things they wanted to do in life, like spending time with their family. They made the right choices, took small steps consistently and paired this with the right mindset when approaching everyday life.

Slow and steady wins the race every time.

So, to make sure you take the right steps in the right direction, I want you to begin by imagining your perfect work day. Think about what your ideal routine is on this perfectly normal day.

What time do you get out of bed?

Where do you have breakfast?

What do you need to get ready for the day?

Who do you speak to first?

When do you take breaks, and what do you do during them?

Do you have a team, or are you working solo?

What makes the clients you work with perfect?

When do you finish for the day?

How do you feel when you've finished working?

By picturing your perfect work day, you can clearly see the habits you can start or improve on. These are the little things that you can do right now that will move you closer to success.

Opening your thoughts to making this happen will influence your actions and how you show up. When your habits are positive, so will the outcomes for your business. And when your mindset aligns with those positive habits, you will be much closer to accomplishing your dreams.

Making small adjustments in your daily habits will help you implement gradual changes to how you structure your day and organize your time. These little changes will incrementally support the next stage of growth in your coaching business and make that perfect work day a reality.

Action 3: Check where your business is today

Let me ask you a question: How is your business doing right now?

Be completely honest with your answer because you can't

move ahead if you don't first appreciate where you are.

By checking the status of your coaching business, you can better assess your reality, review your strengths and weaknesses, and identify your key focus areas. If you know what's missing, you can do something about it in a planned and intentional way. But if you don't know where the gaps are, you can't plan. So, you need to take the time to get clear on your starting point.

You do this by conducting an audit of your business. Go over each aspect of it, from your goals, mission and vision, systems and automation, marketing, finances, and even your passion for the work.

Then ask yourself which of these you need to work on more and which achievements you are proud of. Recognise what you found hard to do and what you learned from each experience.

Action 4: Create a roadmap

Once you know where your focus should be and your business's current reality, you can build your roadmap.

Your roadmap shouldn't just be a static A-Z list because businesses need to be fluid and reactive to new situations or circumstances. Therefore, the roadmap I use in my own business and encourage my clients to use is a 90-day cycle of review-plan-act-review-adjust. This powerful system lets you stay on track and gives you the best chance of achieving your big annual targets. This annual plan, broken into smaller cycles, allows you to continuously align and adjust your actions as you go through the year.

We know the world is unpredictable and turbulent. As an entrepreneur, you need to be agile and adaptable. A 90-day cycle allows you to review, pivot, and plan in shorter chunks while keeping one eye on the end target. No matter what external circumstances come your way, you'll always be able to get back on track with your goals.

When it comes to identifying goals, remember to keep them SMART – specific, measurable, achievable, relevant, and time-bound. So, instead of saying that you want to 'increase your number of clients', set your goal as 'convert five leads from email campaign into clients within the next three weeks.'

Clarifying those details will enable you to plan your next actions. Because each goal you set should have an accompanying actionable step that will lead you closer to achieving your targets.

Action 5: Set your financial targets

This next action is about turning your financial aspirations into financial targets. Setting targets isn't plucking a number out of thin air. Instead, it's strategically setting an achievable figure but being flexible to stretch that amount based on your product ladder, past sales, and business projections for the year ahead. You then need to create a clear plan on how you will achieve them.

Let's use an example.

1   Say you want to hit £10,000 of revenue per month. You first need to work out the combination of products you can sell to reach this figure. To give you an accurate idea of what these are, do an analysis of everything you have sold in the past twelve months.

First, list the individual products and offers you've sold. Arrange them in ascending order, with the lowest price at the top and the highest at the bottom.

Next, write down how many unit sales you made for each offer and the corresponding revenue. Which ones had the highest number? Why? Were they more in demand, or did you actively market them more than the others?

After that, assess who your buyers were. Who did you market the products to? Was there a specific demographic that bought the same products?

Then, identify the pain points and client struggles your most frequently sold offer addresses. Look into why that product was more popular. Can your other products be marketed or offered in the same way?

And finally, pinpoint where you found your buyers or how they found you. Did you make yourself visible in the right places for those clients? Refer to your offline and online channels to give you the full picture.

By using this approach, you can devise a practical system for marketing and selling your offers that will generate the money target you want.

Action 6: Step into your Queen Bee role

1

This last action in setting yourself up for success has to do with leadership. You must take your rightful role as the Queen Bee of your coaching business.

Mike Michalowicz presents this great analogy in his book *Clockwork*, comparing a business to a bee hive. He emphasised the relationship between the worker bees and the Queen. A colony exists to serve the Queen, who in turn is the key to the success and survival of the hive. Her essential role is to lay eggs, which the hive then nurtures and grows for the benefit of the colony. The workers cannot allow the Queen to partake in their tasks, or she would become distracted from her key role and the whole colony would suffer and decline.

Within your business, you are the Queen Bee. This means you need to protect your time and attention in order to focus on your essential roles, without which the business will suffer. As an entrepreneur, you have a duty to yourself and to your business to define and protect your own Queen Bee role.

Consider the real-world comparison of an Accident and Emergency (A&E) department in a hospital. It's critical that patients are treated as quickly and effectively as possible. This is achieved by allowing the Queen Bees – the consultants – to function and apply their specialist skills without unnecessary distraction or taking on non-essential activities.

A truly effective A&E allows consultants to concentrate

on only treating patients, giving the highest possible value to the core function. They are not burdened with administrative tasks or functional activities. The team around them (admin staff, nurses, orderlies, junior doctors) have their own critical roles to play. But they all understand that the key is to allow the Queen Bees – the consultants – to apply their skills in saving lives as effectively as possible.

An understaffed or inappropriately deployed A&E department will be inefficient. In this most critical of environments, that puts human lives at risk.

Of course, it's unlikely within your business that if you get distracted from your Queen Bee role, anyone will die. But you must remember that you are the highest-value asset in your business.

Everyone in the company (including you) should recognise this and always focus on allowing you to perform your Queen Bee role to your best ability. And that means not getting caught up in distractions and non-essential tasks that you can otherwise delegate to your employees or freelancers.

Now you have set yourself up for success, it's time to turn your attention to the pillars of your business, which make you unique from every other coach.

1

KEY POINTS

- When you take the time to set yourself up for success, you'll feel more prepared and motivated to work on your business.
    - Action 1: Get in the right mindset
    - Action 2: Adjust your daily habits
    - Action 3: Check where your business is today
    - Action 4: Create a roadmap
    - Action 5: Set your financial targets
    - Action 6: Step into your Queen Bee role

Step #2:

Know the Pillars of Your Business

Your pillars are the foundations of your business. They encompass your brand, story, and message and should shine through in everything you do. Every business needs an identity. When you know what your business stands for, you'll know how and what to communicate. Connections will be formed and credibility built.

2

Know the Pillars of Your Business

When you don't know what makes you different from other coaches, it's hard to create an impact. You won't know what to talk about or how to position what you do, and your business lacks foundations. You will also probably feel like your business has a Sahara-scale client drought.

When my client, Martha, and I started working together, she had incredible knowledge and ideas, but her execution was poor. She hadn't quite figured out how her ideas fitted together and how she could best present them to her audience. This meant her content was all over the place.

So, we worked on taking what was in her head and creating powerful pillars around her zone of genius. We separated her ideas into topics that she presented clearly through models and graphics, so her ideal clients could see exactly what she stood for. She blended this with her own story and allowed her personality to shine through.

Her words resonated deeply with her ideal clients, and

2

they could see she had stood in their shoes and had come through the other side. They trusted that she could help them do the same. She built more relationships with clients and potential clients. She created more trust and connection with the people she spoke to and established cohesion in her marketing.

All of these, put together, gave Martha genuine opportunities to make an impact on her clients and coaching business. Consequently, she began attracting her ideal clients, and her Sahara-scale client drought ended.

Knowing the pillars of your business is knowing what you stand for. Simply put, these pillars make you, you. They will allow you to stand head and shoulders above others in your field and show your future clients that you can help them.

People buy from people. Therefore, human connection is key.

Keep in mind that people don't buy coaching – they buy coaches. They pay for the person who will help them get to where they want to be, and they will only do that if they feel a sincere connection to you. Because relatability is everything.

The second step of my Signature Framework is putting the pillars of your business in place. This is all about building your brand from the bottom up. It's ensuring that the foundations exist so you can create a coaching business ready and prepped for success.

Why is defining your pillars so crucial for success?

The reality is every business needs an identity. This is why people buy from you rather than your competitors. It will also make sure that your business stands out and gets noticed.

When you know what your business stands for by defining your business pillars, you'll know how and what to communicate.

You'll be more confident about your brand identity and the personality of your business. You'll become more secure about the story you want to tell, your message, and what's unique about you. Also, you'll be able to expertly communicate what you do and why people should work with you.

Defining your success pillars shouldn't be an overwhelming and complex process, and you can do it by following these four simple actions.

Action 1: Define your brand

To establish yourself as someone prominent in your field or to market anything, you first need to define your brand.

Your brand forms the basis of your marketing efforts and strategies. It helps you develop relationships and loyalty, both essential in building your business.

Think of your brand as your identity and how your audience and customers perceive you. It is the face behind your business and what people say about you when you're not in the room. Businesses that don't have a well-defined brand risk being unidentifiable in a crowded space. Instead, you want people to instantly recognise your business.

2

Your brand identity includes how your business appears, the tone of voice you use for your business, how your business is perceived, and its overall feel. These elements create the unique tone and aesthetics you want to project. As your business evolves, so too will your brand and identity.

Your brand is the personality of your business. It's what you want people to think and feel when they encounter you. From the colours and fonts you use, to the communication you put out there, verbal and nonverbal, all reflect your brand.

Small businesses often leave their brand work until they've got their business figured out. But the brand work is part of figuring it all out. Creating a brand isn't just about the pretty colours, fonts, and logos (and you don't need a logo to have a successful personal brand – I don't know any client who chose a coach because of her logo!). Branding shouldn't be something you do later because it's the foundation your entire business is built on.

The key to great branding is consistency. A good way to make sure that your brand is consistent throughout all your marketing materials, messaging, online channels, and everywhere, is by creating a branding document.

In your branding document, you can define the colours, fonts, scaling, and proportions of your content. It's a great reminder for you when generating new content and can really help when you outsource work. It will also aid your virtual assistant (VA) or social media manager to create content that's consistent and aligned with your brand.

Remember that even though consistency is important,

your brand isn't fixed. It will evolve as your business develops, and in the future, a rebrand can be a powerful way to grab your audience's attention.

2

Action 2: Tell people about your business pillars and what your business stands for

When it comes to deciding your pillars, they can be anything you want. Your pillars might be based on your values, powerful words that tell people what they'll get from working with you, or simply on the types of services you offer. But whatever you choose, they should be integral to your business, and you should get excited about sharing them.

If you want values such as integrity, trust, and compassion to come across in your brand, you need to tell people. Or if there are words that resonate with you, such as clarity, confidence and courage, people need to hear about them.

Creating a strong identity starts with knowing how you're different and making sure people know it. I love creating models and frameworks that paint a powerful picture, as this is often easier than trying to pull it together in sentences and paragraphs (anyone who has worked with me knows I am a big fan of using simple diagrams to explain complex ideas).

The visuals you create and the names of your programmes and offers can be shared in all sorts of places – on your website, social media content, sales pages, and even when you talk to people about your business. The key is to actually share them. This way, you can show the pillars you have defined with greater confidence and attract more people.

2

Action 3: Share your story with authenticity

Your story is unique, and no one else will have exactly the same one.

In business, especially when you're starting, it can be difficult to find your true voice – to understand and feel comfortable with what your business represents and stands for. Often this results in replicating what other coaches are doing in the hope it will build your business faster. However, this approach rarely works. People will buy from you because it's you. In the same way, people will buy from others because it's them.

People buy coaches, not coaching. They need to feel they're understood, and there must be a human connection for a client to work with a coach.

We might feel uncomfortable about sharing our stories, but relatability is key in business. It's what makes the difference between clients observing you or deciding to invest in you.

Authenticity is a big part of this. When you show people the real you – the face behind the brand – you'll build a stronger connection. This is particularly true if you can talk about how you might have once been in their shoes and navigated past it.

There are three types of story you can share with your audience:

> *Your purpose story:* What you do to help clients, your mission and vision as a coach, and the positive changes you want your clients to achieve by working with you.

> *Your founder's story:* How you got started with coaching and built your business. Clients will find you more relatable when they know a bit more about the challenges and achievements you had along the way.

> *Your unforgettable story:* The reasons why your clients stick with you. This might be down to the values or opinions you share. You might stand for something different or have a strong view on something. It's these nuances that make you stick.

People look for common ground, a connection and alignment, and storytelling allows you to use your personal journey to connect, inspire and become known for what you do. When you bring this into the communication of your business, be it written or spoken, you'll build relationships faster. This starts by being authentic in the stories you tell.

Action 4: Get clear on your messaging

To be seen as an authority in your field and grow a following in whatever you do, one thing is vital. You need to know the outcomes you help people to achieve.

It's imperative you know this inside out and can convey it to the people you're talking to. If you know you can help your audience but haven't told them, or you've told them in a way that doesn't resonate, you won't convert your followers into clients.

Your messaging is your business interface. It's the link that sits between you and the people you want to work with.

The key to successful selling and building a responsive and engaged community is to be outstanding at describing what you do and take this one step further by always showing what it really means for your audience.

To do this, try applying the 'So what?' test.

If people can still respond to you with 'So what?', you haven't yet reached the real benefit.

For example, if you're a virtual assistant and offer a social media scheduling service, consider how this helps your clients. What is the benefit to them? What you sell is the feature, but you always need to talk about the benefit.

In this example, the benefit could be one of several things:

It saves them time (to do what?).

It gives them a stronger online presence that will result in more clients.

It takes the stress away from them.

With your help, they can then focus on the parts of their

business that are more important.

The best way to find out what the benefits are for your audience is to ask them. We can guess, and in most cases, we'd have a good idea, but don't join the dots and assume you know if you haven't asked.

When your messaging is clear, your clients will pay for your solution. People don't buy the best products and services – they buy what they can understand.

I like to use this simple structure to help clients build their marketing message.

You help WHO, achieve WHAT, by HOW?

Or

You help WHO, achieve WHAT, without WHAT?

For example, 'I help coaches systemise their processes and make more sales through leveraging effective technology and tools.'

Or, 'I help coaches drive more enquiries into their business without paid advertising.'

This defines:

- Who your ideal clients are and what group or niche they belong to.
- What specific problem your ideal clients want resolved or the outcome you can help them achieve.
- How you can resolve your client's problems through a specific service or product that you offer *or* without the very thing that's stopping them from achieving the result.

If you're having trouble crafting your marketing message

like these examples, try answering this simple question: Your clients are buying the promise of what? Remember, great marketing messages are short, simple, and memorable.

2

With your pillars in place, apply this knowledge to the product or service you offer and the problem it solves. Communicating the benefits of what you offer is key, and in the next chapter, we cover your messaging around it.

KEY POINTS

- Knowing the pillars of your business is knowing what you stand for. They will allow you to stand head and shoulders above others in your field and show your future clients that you can help them.

  - Action 1: Define your brand
  - Action 2: Tell people about your business pillars and what your business stands for
  - Action 3: Share your story with authenticity
  - Action 4: Get clear on your messaging

2

Step #3: Understanding Your Product or Service and the Problem it Solves

No matter what your business creates, you must know how you help people. Otherwise, your messaging will be unclear, and you won't attract clients. This doesn't mean listing all the features of what you sell. It's about recognising and communicating the outcomes, transformations, and benefits people will get from working with you.

Understanding Your Product or Service and the Problem it Solves

3

This third step is where you'll dig deep and connect with who your ideal clients are and how you can help them. Even if you think you know this, we'll go deeper. From this, we'll craft your unique message so it's compelling and speaks the language of your perfect clients so they feel understood.

Being able to articulate who you help and, crucially, what you help them achieve (this second part is often missed) is a must in your business. Because without this, you're speaking to an empty room.

What we cover in this chapter is one of the most important exercises you'll ever do as a business owner. Getting clear on the outcome you provide is often the biggest sticking point most people have in their business. Without clarity on who you want to work with and how you help them, it is likely you won't reach the right people, and your message won't be heard.

Using platitudes, generalized terms, or communicating in the same way as everyone else won't enable you to stand out and stand tall. Your people need to know the specific outcome you help them create.

If you're a coach who works with clients on many different things because it's client-led, that's okay too. You can still perfect a killer offer that shows people exactly why you're the person to help them find the result they want.

To give you a clearer picture of how you can do this, let me share a story about one of my clients. Kelly came from a corporate background, and wanted to move from consulting to coaching. Despite nearly two decades of professional experience, she got stuck and lost her spark. She knew what kind of change she wanted to see in her business but wasn't sure if she could make it happen. I helped her become clear on what her ideal clients needed, and we built a suite of offers around this.

We refined her outcome to be specific and clear so that hiring her would become an easy decision for the people with the problem she could solve. In other words, clients could immediately see the outcomes of her offer, hear her message, and trust her to help them.

When all of this came together, Kelly took a giant leap forward and regained her confidence. She reconnected with her spark and made the changes she wanted in her business. She successfully achieved her business objectives, such as identifying her niche, developing and testing her product offers, and launching a signature programme. The result was that she quickly booked her first clients for her new premium programme. Kelly moved away from being stuck by understanding the outcomes of her offer from her ideal clients' perspectives.

Making your clients feel understood is a must in any business, but especially in coaching.

People often skip talking about the outcome the client wants, yet this is the most important thing to emphasise. This happens because the outcome is much harder to define and it's easier to talk about the stepping stones to the outcome than the outcome itself.

Let me give you an example.

A coach tries to sell a coaching package that will provide clarity on career goals. What we need to answer is when a client has clarity on their career goals, what will they be able to do that they can't do now? The clarity isn't the destination. It's just a stepping stone. What we need to be able to do is define what this clarity will bring:

A promotion?

A pay rise?

A career change?

Ultimately, they don't want the clarity – they want what the clarity will give them.

The stepping stone isn't worth anywhere near as much as the outcome, and when you sell the outcome, you'll command a much higher rate because the transformation is greater. Therefore, don't fall short of offering what your clients are really looking for.

How to Define Your Niche

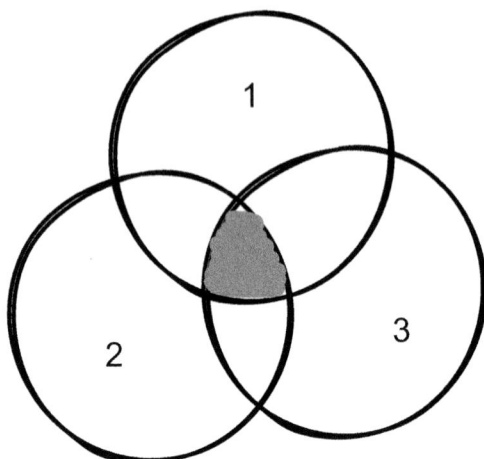

One of the hardest things for coaches to do in the early stages of their business is to define their niche. Your niche is really important because it shapes your entire marketing message and the foundations of your business.

The three circles above stand for enjoyment, impact and, finally, where the gap or need in the market is that can be monetized.

When my clients are struggling to find their niche, I ask them three questions.

1. What do you love doing in your business?

    This is about enjoyment. We have to design a business that we love. By focusing on what you love doing and working with the people you love working with, you'll create an incredible business that lights you up.

2. What are you good at, and where can you help to

bring the best results?

> This is about impact and results. It makes sense to work within your zone of genius because that way you'll create the most amazing testimonials and raving fans. Where do your true strengths lie?

3. Who will pay you for the results?

> This is about getting paid! You're running a business, not a hobby. Make sure you remember that.

The 3 Actions to Understanding Your Product or Service and the Problem it Solves

It is essential in any business to articulate who you help and, more importantly, what you help them to achieve.

Your clients will feel understood and it will demonstrate that you're the right person to help them. Below are the three simple actions to take to understand your products and services and what outcomes your clients can expect from them.

Action 1: Differentiate features from benefits and understand the importance of outcomes

A feature is your product or service. The benefit is what this means to, or gives, your client. This is what you should talk about in all of your communications. This is the outcome.

It's about them, not you. What exactly are they looking for, and how can you ensure they know you can help? This is an example of leading with the outcome.

Your certifications, background, and services only come second to potential clients. The thing they are most concerned with is the problem they have and their desired outcome. Therefore, everything you do should centre around this.

I'm a qualified coach with a distinction, yet in all the years I've run my business, no one has ever asked me a) whether I'm qualified or b) what grade I got. Why? Because they are looking for someone to help them grow their business – this is their primary driver. They don't care about my qualifications; they are focused on the results I can help them achieve and who else I've helped.

You might be concerned that it's hard for you to think in terms of outcomes. Don't worry if you are – many people initially find this difficult.

To communicate with and sell to your target audience, first understand what your ideal clients need. If you can communicate with your potential clients and customers in their language, they are more likely to notice and buy from you.

When you do this, their 'problem' becomes visible, and their awareness is raised by exposing their pain points and headaches. Remember you're also demonstrating to them that you have a solution to their problem. Clients will pay for the solution if your message is clear and compelling.

When you can clearly communicate the outcomes that you provide, you are making yourself stand out among competitors. This is because you are speaking in a language your audience understands. You are answering the question, 'How will this person's life be different after working with you?'

On the other hand, you also need to avoid selling your offer without acknowledging why your potential customers might need it. Here's what I mean:

"Would you like to buy my coaching?"

"Here's a special offer."

"New package launching."

In other words, these are all 'Me, me, me.'

Remember, it's about them, not you.

Please don't fall into the second trap of diving straight into the thing you're selling and missing the reasons someone should buy. Otherwise, they'll scroll on by.

Instead, here's how to position your coaching, consulting, or service the correct way:

1.   Attract the right people by first talking about the things that matter to them. What's not working, their frustrations, and their desires. You can say things like:

> "Are you working all hours in your business but not making enough money?"
>
> "Are you sick and tired of seeing other people do well, yet you're stuck?"
>
> "What difference would achieving X make to your life?"

3

2. Use their words. Describe how they feel. Ask them these questions:

    "Is it getting you down?"

    "Are you wondering how long you can keep it going?"

    "Do you start each day with a knot in your stomach?"

3. Get them to identify what will happen if they don't fix things.

4. Help them to paint a picture of what life could be like, such as:

    "Working fewer hours and enjoying family time."

    "Enough money coming in each month to hire a social media manager."

    "Being able to go on holiday and still get paid."

    "Feeling confident and excited for the future with a clear strategy."

    "More money than your corporate job."

5. Offer them a stepping stone to making this happen. Your solution is the bridge from where they are (A) to where they want to go (B).

    "Here's how we can make this happen."

    "Here's a link to book a free call."

    "Let's see if we can create [insert solution]."

6. Tell them about your coaching, highlighting how it will help them.

3

Notice the first five points are about THEM, and only the last one is about YOU. So many people are missing the opportunity to build interest and are diving straight into their offer without setting the scene.

How to Craft Powerful Messaging

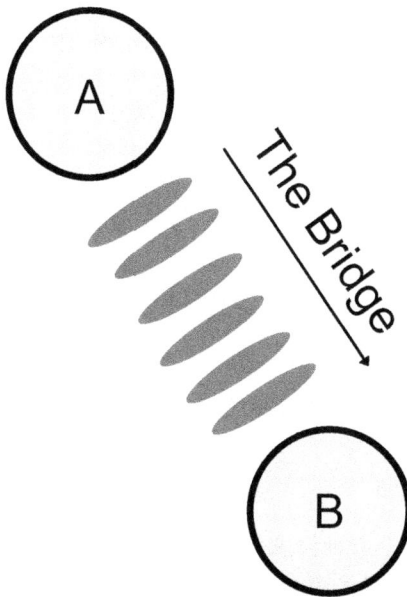

A

The Bridge

B

This exercise helps create a clear, concise and compelling marketing message that literally speaks the language of your ideal clients. Your primary role as a coach is to help people move from A to B via the path (the bridge) of least resistance, where A is where they are now, and B is where they want to get to.

It's easy to fall into the trap of talking about your services, offer, programme, workshop, or course and then wonder why no one is buying. People are looking for answers to their problems. They don't care so much about how they get there. Their primary concern is finding a solution.

So, when you talk about the thing you sell rather than the solution or outcome, you miss the mark. It doesn't resonate because that's not what your clients are looking for. Think of your service as the stepping stone to the solution instead. It is the vehicle that will get them there. You're giving them the promise of what?

Here's a quick exercise that will help you:

1. First, get clear on their big problem. Perhaps it's even their living hell. The relationship they're trapped in. The business that isn't making any money, the life they don't love. How is this affecting their life, and what will happen if they don't fix it?

2. Next, think about what they'd rather have instead. What is the result they'd give anything to have? What is their heaven? How will their life change? What is this worth to them?

3. Now, think of your service as the stepping stones from A to B. From their living hell to their wonderful heaven. This is your signature framework.

Remember, you're selling the outcome – the result, not the steps. Don't fall into the trap of only talking about the service – people buy the outcome. Map this out for your business and notice the shift in thinking.

Action 2: Know what it takes for people to know, like, and trust your brand

Being known – or visible – is being in the right places for your ideal clients and adopting a consistent approach to building the visibility of your personal brand. The more visible you are, the more you will be noticed. This leads, in turn, to more interest in your work and more enquiries and sales.

You could be the best at what you do, but if too few people know about it, you won't get far.

The second thing is that to buy from you, people have to not just like you, but LOVE you. That means sharing content that people want to see, spending time getting to know them and understanding what they need from you and how you can give value.

Of course, it's not possible that everyone will like you, and that's okay. We're not in business to be liked by everyone. We're in business to be liked by the people who matter most. These are the people whose lives, businesses or situations you can really make a difference to. This is why understanding your ideal client is so important because it's much easier to create content for them than to create it for everyone.

Thirdly, we need to build trust. This takes the relationship element one step further. People won't buy from you just because they know about you or like you. People buy from people they trust.

Trusting you is when they believe that you are the person

to help them. You might demonstrate this through sharing testimonials or other social proof or being credible or an authority in your field. When you offer valuable support and are open, honest and transparent, trust is grown. This is one of the biggest determining factors as to whether people will buy from you.

3   Action 3: Craft your mission statement

A detailed mission statement will serve as the foundation for everything you do next in your business, and there will be no more doubts or concerns about your niche or unique selling point. Therefore, this is one of the most important exercises you'll do as a business owner.

Without clarity on who you want to work with and how you'll serve people, you'll feel stuck and unable to drive your business forward. Therefore, it's essential you are clear on your message in order to build connections and generate sales.

Your words are vitally important in attracting the right people and communicating how you can help them. They need to know you're the exact person for them, and it's up to you to tell them.

This mission statement is something that you will not share with anyone other than yourself. It is your personal blueprint. And it's something you should remind yourself of every day because you need to be clear about who you help, how you help them, and what results they get.

A mission statement can also guide your communication and messaging – from what you post on social media to what you write on your website and how you describe what you do for people you meet.

To create your mission statement, work through the nine questions below.

- Question #1: *What problem do you solve?*

    Define one problem your product or service solves, such as lose weight, too few clients, or reduce feeling overwhelmed. If you work with more than one problem, that's fine. Just choose the biggest problem your clients face.

- Question #2: *Who do you solve that problem for? (Or who do you help to solve that problem for themselves?)*

    If you work with different types of people, choose one for now. For example, if you help people to get a better work-life balance, who is that person? Mums, entrepreneurs, school teachers?

- Question #3: *Is the problem you solve a severe problem?*

    The more severe it is, the higher the price people will pay for a solution. You will need to consider whether they can afford your prices. For example, if you help people to get a new job, C-suite professionals might be more likely to afford your services than university graduates.

- Question #4: *What labels can you apply to the people you've defined above?*

  Who are they? What are their character traits, which types of people do you love working with? For example, ambitious, determined, respectful, action takers. Write five character traits your ideal clients possess.

- Question #5: *What are the character traits of the people who aren't your ideal clients and customers?*

  Knowing who you love working with is one thing, being clear on who you don't is another! Think about the character traits of people that are not right for you. What makes them less than ideal?

- Question #6: *What keeps your clients awake at night?*

  What is their living hell? Or if it's not this extreme, what is causing them frustration or challenges? Put yourself in their shoes if you need to. If it's a living hell for them, how is this situation affecting their life, relationships, family, and health? What will happen if they don't solve it?

- Question #7: *How will their life change with your help?*

  Write this in detail. What will they be able to do that they can't now? What new superpowers will they have? Not just more energy, but more energy to do what? Play with their grandchildren? More money, but for what?

3

> This needs to be specific. What is their heaven?

- Question #8: *What's the consequence if they don't make this change?*

  > If their life stays as it is, what will happen? What will they have to settle for? What will they be saying to themselves? What's the secondary impact of this on their family and relationships?

- Question #9: *Can you pull this all into a mission statement? (Of course, you can!)*

  > Just fill out the below to make your mission statement:
  >
  > I help WHO [insert type of client] to achieve or solve WHAT [insert biggest problem] by how or without [insert consequence].

3

Now you have a mission statement remember that this is for you, not your clients. It's to give you clarity on the people you help and how you help them.

With this mission statement in mind, you are ready to create irresistible offers for your future clients.

Key Points

3

- Being able to articulate who you help
  and, crucially, what you help them
  achieve, is a must. Clarity on outcomes
  is often the biggest sticking point most
  people have in their business; without
  this it is likely you won't reach the right
  people, and your message won't be
  heard.
    - Action 1: Differentiate features
      from benefits and understand the
      importance of outcomes
    - Action 2: Know what it takes for
      people to know, like, and trust
      your brand
    - Action 3: Craft your mission
      statement

Step #4:

Creating Irresistible Offers

If you only offer one way people can work with you, you risk losing potential clients who like you but don't like your offer. A couple of well-thought-out revenue streams at different price points allow you to meet your clients at any stage or level in their business. You can then step them through your services and programmes as they grow. It's not where they start – it's where they end up that matters.

Creating Irresistible Offers

There was a time, a few years into my business, when my diary was jam-packed pretty much every day. It was almost the end of me.

4

I was overrun with clients. I had more clients than I knew what to do with – an amazing situation on the one hand, but on the other, I'd created a monster in my own business. It stole my time, stopped me from looking after myself and constantly overwhelmed me. The worst thing was that it was all my own fault.

I grew the monster and didn't notice what was happening before it was almost too late. As if that wasn't bad enough, I was working all hours with no prospect of further growth because I'd literally filled every corner of my diary.

The clients were lovely. The situation wasn't.

I knew something had to change, but I was holding back from making that change because I thought (incorrectly) that stopping and creating a different business model would cause my revenue to go down – and I didn't want it to. Also, I was too busy to stop and change. I felt I couldn't.

The catalyst to do something different was a family

holiday where I spent time doing coaching calls rather than being on the beach with my kids. I did the calls because I didn't have anywhere to move them to. The weeks before and after were already jam-packed. After the holiday, I carved out time to look at what I was doing and created my first group programme.

I stepped people into a group format and have never looked back.

Being too busy to take your foot off the pedal and make key business decisions is not running a business. It's being in the back seat of your business and letting it run you. It's absolutely possible to change your business model and see your revenue skyrocket. It's also absolutely possible to have time and happy clients.

If you're in this situation right now, and feel like there are not enough hours in the day because you have too many clients, then I urge you to look at creating a group programme. I think you'll never look back.

Not everyone will be at the 'overrun with clients' stage yet, and that's why we need to have a selection of offers to cater for every client who comes our way. So, in the fourth step of my Signature Framework, we'll be looking at how to build out a suite of offers that work together and complement each other.

The 3 Actions to Creating Irresistible Offers

The most sustainable businesses have a range of revenue streams. Packaging your services into irresistible offers will help you look at new ways to generate revenue that enables you to reach higher income levels. You'll do this through leveraging the power of other business models and building out a product ladder in your business that meets your client's needs.

This step will allow you to focus on the products and services you sell and how they fit into the spectrum of what your clients want versus the best business model for you.

4

Similar to how I shifted from a 1:1 model to a group programme, you too can take advantage of this approach to structure your offers, so you have the best chance to catch the clients that come your way. The best thing about this is you don't have to reach breaking point with the number of clients you have to implement this; you can do it much earlier.

If you only have 1:1 coaching to offer people, you will eventually reach a point where you are at capacity and lose the opportunity of a new client to another coach. The people who reach out to you still have a need, and they will undoubtedly find another way to satisfy that need if you can't deliver.

The other benefit to having multiple packages, particularly for newer coaches, is that people who come to you might be unable to afford your 1:1 coaching. This is where there is the opportunity to create other types of offers even if you don't have many clients at the moment.

If your offers are packaged irresistibly for clients, and you give them a choice by meeting them where they are at, they're more likely to grab the chance to work with you right away.

Below are the three actions to packaging irresistible offers:

Action 1: Have a signature framework for how you help your clients

Having a 'signature system', 'framework' or a 'methodology' for how you help your clients will give you a huge step up because it helps you to become known for something more quickly, and therefore you will get more client enquiries. It will also give you unbelievable clarity over what you stand for, the work you do, how you communicate this, and the content you should create.

Let's think about it for a moment. You want to be known in your field as someone credible who helps people get results. You want people to know about you, recommend you to others, and you want to be seen. For any of this to be possible, you must clearly demonstrate what you are known for and how you help people. Being known as a 'coach', 'photographer' or 'virtual assistant' isn't enough in the competitive online space.

But it gets better. When you've established your framework, you'll be able to roll it out in different ways, at different price points, to meet the needs of more people. You will have something to offer everyone who comes your way without creating more work for yourself, as it's all the same – it's just delivered in different ways. Some of it will be in more depth, for example, as a 1:1 client session, or it might be a top slice of this if it's in a membership.

What we are working our way through now in this book is my signature framework, as I apply these steps in all the work that I do in flexible ways depending on the intensity and format of the coaching relationship. Your framework is simply the steps you take your clients through from A to B – from where they are now to where they want to get to.

To craft your signature framework, think about the clients you have and what you help them with. What's the biggest thing they need help with? What's the one thing they need to fix most of all? What are they typing into Google searching for the answers to? Is there a pattern?

Think about the clients you've worked with already. Do you always cover the same topic at the start, and does this lead to an obvious next step? Do the same questions come up? Can you map out the workflow and apply this, even loosely, to each person you work with?

This is an opportunity to drill down on the work you love doing and attract more of the kinds of people who need this from you. This is about you being the go-to person to help with their problems and your signature offer is the vehicle through which their transformation is delivered.

For example, if your work is bespoke, you may want to keep it as a top-level framework with plenty of scope to

4

tailor it. If, alternatively, you recognise similarities between your clients and you're doing the same thing, even loosely, with each one, there's scope to create a more detailed framework.

Once you're clear on your signature framework, it's now time to turn it into a powerful graphic. We've all heard the phrase 'a picture is worth a thousand words'. You need to bridge your framework and turn it into an eye-catching visual that clearly shows people the path you'll take them on when they work with you (and remember to show the outcomes and benefits because this is what sells!).

4

Action 2: Build a product ladder

Once you have a signature framework that gives you clarity on your zone of excellence and clearly shows people the work you do, you have incredible flexibility with how you apply it.

Think about how you like to work.

Are you a people person, and do you love groups? Or would you say you're more introverted and prefer to be behind the scenes? Do you love making videos or running live events? Do you get excited about tech? Or do you avoid it at all costs? This information will guide you in creating the product ladder based on your framework and enables you to bring together the elements of your business that you adore.

To begin this process, you're going to initially have three

levels of offers in your product ladder: low-range, mid-range, and high-range. Think about your offers and how you can create these three options. What will distinguish your high-range price point from something lower? Not everyone is looking for the same solution, and having choices means more flexibility with how you work with people and more money coming into the business.

The Product Ladder

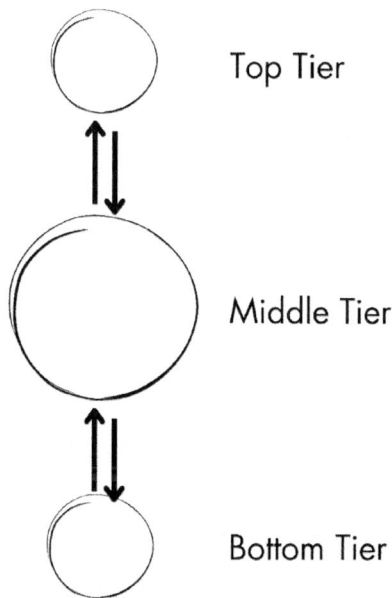

Top Tier

Middle Tier

Bottom Tier

4

One of the smartest things I did early on in my business was create a product suite of offers that served my audience where they were at. This ensured I could support them at every step of their journey, from just starting out and making a few thousand per month, to growing fast and then scaling up from there. However you help your clients, whether in the business, health, wellbeing, career, executive, or life coaching niches, your clients need different things at different times.

A few months into my business, I realised this. It was a monumental moment for me and changed everything. I built a product suite, and this is what started to happen...

People stepped in at the bottom, they had a taste of what it was like to work with me, they started seeing fantastic results, and slowly but surely, they worked through from the bottom to the top. They stayed with me, and it became much less about one-time offers and much more about lifetime value and client retention.

If you're selling one-time offers, you'll end up chasing clients every month, and this is unsustainable, exhausting and slow. When you have something to offer people that gives them what they need, and they repeat buy, you start reaching higher revenue months.

Your product ladder or offer suite is a hugely important part of the process, and it's something that isn't often thought out well enough. It's so easy to do what you see others doing, offer one thing or offer too many random things without being strategic. Too much choice for your clients is as bad as too little choice.

There has to be an obvious solution for exactly where they are on their journey, and the positioning, creation and marketing of this requires planning.

Do you have a product suite that steps people into working with you at every different level?

When you get this right, you get more enquiries, generate more sales, create more impact, and experience fast growth.

Another thing to note is that the offers in your product ladder should always be based on your financial targets and external circumstances. For example, if you have a goal to earn £10,000, £20,000 or any other amount per month, you need to make sure you're offering the right combinations to get you there. Selling a £49 tripwire, even in high volumes, is probably going to leave you short.

Also, consider your time. If you're working in a 9-5 and building your business on the side, your available time will impact what you sell and how long it takes to deliver.

4

Action 3: Work out your pricing strategies

It can be hard to work out how to price your products and services. Do you pluck a number out of thin air, hoping it's in the right ballpark? Or use a system that's more calculated based on your time?

In either case, it has to be something people are willing to pay for the promise it offers.

That said, how you present your prices is something you need to consider in greater detail. I advise you to look at the following structure through the lens of your experiences as a purchaser, as well as a business owner.

Deciding your pricing can be a tricky thing to get right. Too low and you find yourself working like a dog with no time to develop your business. Worse still, your clients may not value your work, and you'll attract the wrong kinds of clients. Too low is definitely not good, but neither is too high.

You can't sell high ticket if you haven't built your reputation and credibility. Or if you don't have an audience of high-ticket buyers. You need to get the momentum going, and the only way to do this is with paying clients and customers.

If you're pricing yourself out of the market, your bottom line will suffer, and your testimonials will be few and far between. It's chicken and egg because the social proof will help you get more clients. You might feel like your business is going at a snail's pace, which isn't good for your confidence. You need clients and customers to grow.

So, what's the right price point?

A good barometer is to ask yourself if you would invest in your own services at the price you're offering them because often, we are our own ideal client.

It's the first number in your price – in other words, the leading number – that is important. People will consider the difference between £49 and £50 far greater than only £1 because the first number they see is a 4 versus a 5. The second number – the trailing number – is much less important.

Bearing this in mind, look at what you're selling currently and list them on a piece of paper.

Do you have products for £63 that you could be selling for £69? Perhaps a monthly membership that's £21 per month could be £27? Or a tripwire that's £31 and could be £39 instead?

Apply this in reverse, too, when you offer discounts. If the leading number is the one that's important in terms of buyer psychology, a price reduction from £95 to £89 will be more appealing than £99 to £93.

So, instead of focusing on the trailing number, prioritise the leading number.

And when it comes to presenting your special offers to your audience, be sure to give them the highest number between the money off they'll get versus the percentage discount.

Here's an example:

You have a new group programme that you're offering a 20% reduction incentive for people to test as a pilot. The programme would ordinarily be £1,500 and with 20% off it comes to £1,200 instead.

The saving is £300, which has more impact than 20%. It's the bigger number for a start, but also, people tend to pay less attention to the % quoted unless it's a huge % off.

In marketing, it's also common to present the item you want to sell alongside a much more expensive item.

For example, position the price of your group programme alongside your most expensive 1:1 option. Or your mid-range option alongside your top-of-the-range item. The mid-range service might be £1,500, but your most expensive bespoke service is £6,000. This makes the mid-range seem like a bargain.

The person considering working with you may have disregarded the group programme as too expensive, but when presented in the context of your 1:1 bespoke service, it becomes more affordable.

By following these three actions – create a signature system, build a product ladder, and work out your pricing strategies

– you will have irresistible offers your clients can choose from. You'll generate consistent results from different revenue streams in your business and cater to all your clients' needs.

In the next chapter, we'll cover how you can build more predictable sales by implementing your sales funnel.

4

Key Points

- The most sustainable businesses have a range of revenue streams. Packaging your services into irresistible offers will help you look at new ways to generate revenue that enables you to reach higher income levels.
    - Action 1: Have a signature system for how you help your clients
    - Action 2: Build a product ladder
    - Action 3: Work out your pricing strategies

4

Step #5:
Building Consistent, Predictable Revenue

If there is no consistency or predictability around when clients come into your business, you cannot plan or forecast for the future. This could leave you with a feast and famine situation where some months are amazing and others terrible. Unpredictable revenue is one of the biggest dangers in any business. Introducing a smart sales funnel can change this. Your sales funnel comprises the steps people take from when they first become aware of you, to becoming a customer.

Building Consistent, Predictable Revenue

J ackie was a client of mine who had started an online coaching business. During the early stages, she had a good influx of clients. And because of this, she got busier and busier.

The problem was that she was on the revenue roller-coaster – a good month followed by a bad one. This created a whole manner of issues in her business, including an inability to accurately forecast and not being able to confidently pay for things. And it played havoc with her mindset.

This was because her business model bottlenecked clients who wanted to start her programme straightaway. When these clients finished her programme, Jackie had to scramble to find new clients, but the number who signed up wasn't always the same.

All of Jackie's time, energy, and resources were spent on finding and managing clients. Consequently, she no longer had the headspace to think about the next steps for her business. It became more about surviving her client sessions day

5

to day.

Jackie had hit a plateau. She was no longer planning ahead and forecasting her revenue and growth. Yes, she was getting clients. But the inconsistency of the results meant that something had to change.

So, Jackie needed to pause and think about what her next quarter was going to be like. What was her message? And what should be her marketing strategy moving forward so she could escape inconsistent revenues?

As we began working together, we identified what Jackie was doing that prevented her reaching her revenue goals. It was clear all her busy work with clients wasn't pushing her business forward. In truth, all the busy work steals the creativity, innovation, and planning needed to go into building your business. This leads to your business stagnating unless you make a change. But making that change is hard because there's the fear you'll lose money and clients.

The most sustainable businesses have a range of revenue streams. We've all heard the line that the average millionaire has seven revenue streams. You should think about your business in the same way. Putting all your eggs in one basket is risky. Diversifying your income is smart. You can do this by making money from a range of offers. Creating a variety of ways to generate revenue allows you to reach higher income levels by leveraging the power of business models and building out a product ladder for your client's needs.

The 5 Actions to Building Consistent, Predictable Revenue

Clients are at the heart of any great business. This comes from having a brilliant marketing plan and strategy, which ensures you can communicate the benefits of your products and services to the right people at the right time, resulting in business growth.

But I understand that this is not the easiest thing to do. A lot of business owners struggle with inconsistent or unpredictable leads into their pipeline. Not having a reliable lead generation strategy might make you feel frustration and even financial anxiety. You might be working too hard for the money you're earning, resulting in burnout and possibly falling out of love with your business.

The solution to many of these problems depends on the type of business you dream of having.

If you're happy with a bit of pocket money or a couple of thousand each month is enough for you to live the life you want, then you might find the clients you need without much of a strategy.

However, if you have big aspirations and crave more freedom, choices and wealth, you'll need some way of generating leads, and Step Five of the Signature Framework will help. This undoubtedly means having some sort of sales funnel and lead generation strategy for your business because that is how you generate *predictable* sales.

5

Action 1: Realise the potential of the online space

The internet has become such a huge part of our lives it's almost impossible to remember what it was like before. The landscape of business has changed beyond recognition, and the power that's literally at our fingertips is astonishing.

A few decades ago, businesses had to rely on phone calls and mailshots to make sales. The reach was tiny, the costs were huge, and selling outside your local area, never mind internationally, was reserved for big corporates.

The online space we can now access has the power to revolutionise your business. The ability to reach and connect with hundreds or even thousands of people with ease and offer solutions to their problems is mind-blowing.

It's time to think big. It's time to set stretching goals for your business and realise the potential of the online space – what it can do for your business and how it can change your life.

But with so many platforms, how do you know which is the right one?

The first thing to think about is where your ideal clients can be found.

If you're a business that works with retired folk, you might be less likely to find this demographic on Instagram. Likewise, if you work with teenagers, this age group might be less prolific on LinkedIn. So, think about the platform where your ideal clients can be found instead of the one you prefer.

But, at the same time, remember your objective is to be

noticed. Many businesses employ an 'omnipresent' approach to marketing. That is, being seen across many channels so your prospects see you when they open Facebook, Instagram and LinkedIn, for example.

If you have a team or are about to hire one, this *could* work for you. But keep in mind that if you're a one-person band in your business and are doing everything, this will consume your time.

Balance is key, along with picking the best platform for you and being consistent.

Action 2: Understand the power of having a sales funnel

5

The term 'sales funnel' typically refers to the journey a person goes on from finding out about you, your product or your service to ultimately buying from you and becoming a customer. It's the journey potential customers go through on the way to purchase.

This can be applied to any business, but over the years, it's become highly relevant to the online space, where the ability to attract customers in large numbers, and the power that lies at your fingertips in doing so, can have a far-reaching impact on your business.

The top, middle, and bottom of a sales funnel are three typical components. However, the exact steps can change depending on the sales model used by your business.

You start with a lot of potential customers who may have

heard of your product or service.

A smaller part of that group may want to learn more, and an even smaller portion may actually contact you. As the funnel progresses, you speak to fewer but more engaged individuals until you meet those who will become clients.

When it comes to generating sales, it's not enough to post on social media and hope clients arrive. Posting on social media is an important part of the process, but it doesn't stop there. You have to attract the right clients with powerful content that helps them step forward.

The first part of this is finding where your ideal clients are and being visible in the right places. You will then need to talk about what matters most to them so they move closer to you. Finally, provide them with huge value so they convert into paying clients.

Crucially, you must also deliver an incredible service that generates exceptional results and amazing testimonials.

Without an effective sales funnel, you have no control over the flow of enquiries into your business. And if you have no control over the flow of enquiries, you have no control over who will be your next client and how much money you earn. You won't have a reliable way to scale or streamline sales, making it impossible to forward plan and forecast. This is a killer in business and is the number one reason businesses fail.

Action 3: Don't Just Talk to the Dot

Most coaches talk to the dot. The 'dot' pertains to people ready to buy your service now and work with you straight away.

But the problem with talking to the dot is that at any moment, there's only a minority of people ready to buy from you.

What about the people not ready to buy from you today, yet still in the circle you're talking to? These people may be ready to work with you within the next few weeks or months. How would your messaging resonate with them?

This is important to consider because if you're marketing to these people, they need to hear something slightly different to move from viewer to customer. There's a period of time it takes people to know, like, and trust you.

Yes, have a marketing message that talks to the dot, but also stop and think about what other people in your audience need to hear. In addition, make sure your content is moving people through. Because if it's just talking to a specific group, the rest will think your message doesn't resonate with them.

Don't Just Talk to the Dot

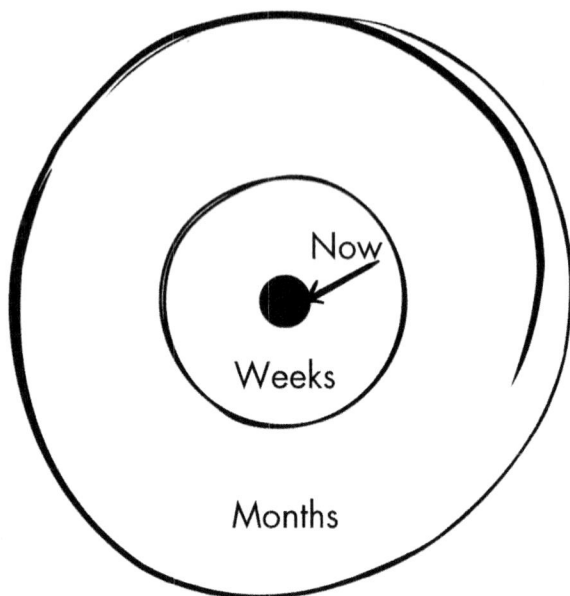

5

Not everyone is in the market to buy from you today. In fact, the number of people ready to jump in now to work with you is small or even tiny if you don't have a large audience.

Instead of spending hours only talking to the people who are in the 'ready camp', how about we also create content that's more strategic and speaks to people who are in the 'not quite ready' camp so they move closer to you more quickly.

What do your 'not quite ready' buyers need to hear from you to get their purses out?

When you can speak to future buyers as well as today's buyers, your audience will grow faster, and you'll get more enquiries.

Action 4: Nail down the elements of a funnel

The steps in a marketing or sales funnel are often referred to as 'AIDA', which stands for Awareness, Interest, Desire and Action. This description of the buyer decision process was first introduced over 100 years ago by John Dewey and Elias St. Elmo Lewis. It is still commonly used today, and the process is separated into four stages:

- Creating Awareness (Attract)

    You need to show people how good you are at what you do and position yourself as the person to help them and offer the solution when the time is right.

    Very simply, it's bringing people into your world and enabling them to take a series of micro-commitments that take them closer to buying.

    There could and should be several ways people can find you. This can be achieved by posting on social media, Facebook Lives, being visible on Instagram, being a guest on someone's podcast, being a guest expert in someone's Facebook group, being in other people's groups, and offering value.

- Creating Interest (Engage)

    Your objective is to encourage people to go one step further. You might offer them valuable content that requires an exchange of their email address, such as a lead magnet, opt-in, or freebie where they make a commitment. They give you their email, which takes them closer to you in your funnel. They're then a subscriber to your email list, and you have the ability to build a relationship with them through your email marketing.

How do you continue to move these people along a little further? You show value, communicate with them, and offer the next step. You must understand your ideal client's needs inside out and communicate this well.

5   •   Creating Desire (Convert)

This is where you turn people from just liking to wanting what you sell. Buying is an emotional process, so it is essential to ensure your ideal clients know how they will benefit from buying your 'thing'. What's in it for them? How will it make their life better?

The steps they might move through in this phase of the funnel could be attending a free webinar or having a discovery call with you. You're setting the stage for them to move forward and buy from you and, at the same time, find the solution they've been looking for.

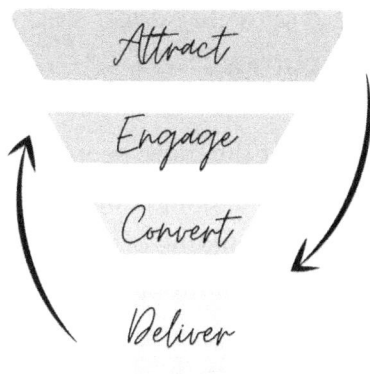

- Creating Action (Deliver your service)

  The action a client takes doesn't necessarily have to end with a sale, although this is the ultimate goal. The action could be any next step you want people to take, such as registering for an event, downloading a brochure, or booking a call. In this case, we'll refer to the action as the point at which the sale is made.

  You have to make it easy for people to say yes and buy from you. This means not over-complicating the options, having clearly laid out sales pages, simple ways to buy, easy ways to pay, and a first-class buyer experience. These are vitally important, and remember that the checkout page is the last point at which people can change their minds.

5

Action 5: Have a plan for each step in your client's buying journey

It stands to reason that the more people you put at the top of your funnel, the more you get out of the bottom. So, if you're only putting a sprinkling of people in at the top, you will only get a tiny number of sales coming through. Quantity is important, but so is quality.

Let's say you are launching a programme and want ten people in it. Your conversion rate could be 10%, so for every ten people you speak to, one will join. This means you need to talk to at least 100 people to find ten people to join. The more people you can take on that journey, the more people will buy from you.

Having a sales funnel brings predictability and consistent income into your business. You need to have a funnel working in the background so you have a steady stream of client enquiries coming into your business because there is nothing worse than having to chase your tail for each new client.

A funnel allows you to take leads through a series of steps toward buying from you. Because when people come into your world, they usually don't buy straight away. They need to get to know you first.

Creating your sales funnel doesn't have to be complicated. It can be as simple as you want. You can have a single funnel that's working well, or multiple funnels that bring you leads from various sources.

As someone who has a coaching or consulting business,

you need to widen your horizons. Have a plan to fill your sales funnel with people who may not be ready to buy today but might explore their options in the future. This is a key component in building a predictable sales pipeline and precisely why we built CoachSpace.ai. We saw that coaches struggled with finding a way to not only generate leads but convert those leads and automate their processes. This is because automation is the key to scaling simply. You can't manage every process yourself. Those who do end up leaving their 9–5 for a 24–7 job, with too few clients and a desperate sense of being overworked and underpaid.

The first part of your funnel is people knowing about you and what you do. This requires you to build visibility, and we'll cover how in the next chapter.

5

KEY POINTS

- If you have big aspirations and crave more freedom, choices and wealth, you'll need a way of generating leads. This means having some sort of sales funnel and lead generation strategy for your business because this is how you generate predictable sales.
  - Action 1: Realise the potential of the online space
  - Action 2: Understand the power of having a sales funnel
  - Action 3: Don't Just Talk to the Dot
  - Action 4: Nail down the elements of a funnel
  - Action 5: Have a plan for each step in your client's buying journey

Step #6:

Building More Visibility

If you're not being seen, you're not able to help people. The people who need you need to know you exist. Your visibility and getting noticed are key. Often, what stops us from creating visibility is worrying about what people will think. The good news is, it's not about you. When you stop making your visibility about you and make it about your ideal clients, being visible feels amazing.

Building More Visibility

When Nicola started her business, she had trouble showing up consistently online. She'd share content if she felt like it, then post nothing for days. Her audience was denied the opportunity to get to know her because she wasn't consistent in building relationships and putting herself out there. She wasn't being seen repeatedly in the right places where, over time, she would become the person her ideal clients would think of when they needed a solution to their particular problem.

6

When Nicola and I started working together, we talked about how the secret to building your business is getting noticed, but this doesn't happen by accident. You can't sit back and hope that people find you, even if you post consistently. You have to be proactive too.

This means going out, finding people and interacting with them. Engaging in their content and putting the time into other people. The opposite of this is sitting back and expecting people to come to you. These conversations changed something in Nicola, and after this, she was off.

The first thing she did was connect with a whole load of

people who shared a similar audience in a non-competing way and arranged a summit online. She organised a panel of speakers and created a brilliant event that catapulted her visibility.

As a result, she gained a ton of new followers through promoting the summit and from the audience of the speakers. Piggybacking off other people's audiences – to your mutual benefit – is a powerful way to boost visibility and gain clients.

Because of her actions, Nicola increased her visibility and drew more potential clients into her sales funnel.

The 5 Actions to Building More Visibility

The simplest way to illustrate why creating an engaged online audience matters, is to describe what it's like not to have one.

- You put content out on social media. Nobody responds. You have no idea if the content is poor, average, or absolutely amazing. Nobody sees it. No one comments or shares.
- You have an idea for an offer but a tiny audience of hard-core cheerleaders, so it's hard to get genuine feedback. You can only guess.
- You put your heart and soul into creating an offer you're certain will transform the lives of those who buy it. But as you have a tiny audience, you only make one or two sales. So, you have no idea if it was

the promotional content that flopped, the sales page was rubbish, or the offer wasn't something people wanted.

If you want to make repeatable sales in your business, you need a big enough pond to fish in. Otherwise, your brilliant work might go unnoticed and it's likely you won't make the sales you want. Building an audience isn't just about finding people to sell your products and services to. You must also build a relationship with those people. This means demonstrating your position and credibility as a coach. It means showing your audience you're the person who can help solve their problem. We will cover all of this in Step Six of the Signature Framework.

Action 1: Use fear as fuel to put yourself out there more

6

Being visible and putting yourself out there can be terrifying. It's scary, often because of judgment and worries about what people will think. But there are a few things to keep in mind.

Firstly, visibility is not vanity. Far from it. It's an essential part of running a modern-day business. People fear being seen and feel more comfortable hiding behind the walls of their office when in reality building a presence is key to the success of their business.

It's true people will talk about you. It's also true people

will judge you. People will think you're big-headed if you talk about what's going well. People will think your business is low-level if you don't talk about your successes. And some people out there will decide they don't like you even when they don't know you.

But others will love you and what you stand for. They'll become your raving fans and tell all of their friends. They'll buy from you and contribute to the growth of your business. These people are the ones you show up for. Who cares about anyone else? Visibility is essential.

The most successful businesses that create the biggest impact show the face behind the brand. This is where people get a sense of the real person and their journey. Overcoming the barriers and beliefs surrounding being visible online is an essential step in your business growth.

Finally, balance the consequence of not acting versus being fearful. Which is worse? What will happen if you don't do anything?

The magic happens outside your comfort zone. Personally commit to pushing your limits, and bit by bit, the uncomfortable will become comfortable.

Action 2: Build an audience organically first

You won't have to worry about losing your audience if you build a strong organic reach that will allow them to firmly identify with your brand. Providing worthwhile content and services will earn people's confidence, which will benefit your business over time.

There are five key ways you can begin leveraging marketing to increase online visibility:

- Collaborate

    One of the best ways to become more visible online is to piggyback or collaborate with people already there and who share the same audience as you. Collaboration in marketing can help increase your online reach, give your brand credibility, and build a network with other highly regarded businesses in your industry.

    For a new coaching business to flourish and survive, developing trust and enduring support is crucial. Collaborative marketing is about growing and forging partnerships for existing businesses.

- Make bold statements

    Making bold statements works wonders for standing out in a competitive market. What industry myths are there that you can strike up conversations about? You can then bust those myths to get more people in front of your content.

    This doesn't mean being so controversial you risk driving away potential customers in your audience. It's more about showing off

6

your brand's unique perspective on a common belief or idea within your industry.

- Start a blog

    Creating free content is the easiest and best way to show off your expertise and drive more traffic to your site. Blogging for your business can also help you become more visible on social media. Every time you write a new piece, you produce information readers may share on social media sites like Instagram, LinkedIn, Facebook, and Pinterest. By doing this, you can advertise your business to possible new clients who may not be familiar with your brand.

    Your blog can also act as a content store rather than constantly putting out original content on your other platforms. You can repurpose material you've already published on your blog and turn it into social media posts, videos, or other types of content.

- Be a guest in other people's communities, audiences and programmes

    This can include blogging, podcast interviews, and free training in other people's Facebook groups. Guest blogging is crucial since it enables you to network with others in your field, present your brand to a new audience, increase website referral traffic, position yourself as an industry thought leader, and maybe create backlinks that will improve traffic to your website.

What can you share with other people's audiences to get more eyes on you?

- Paid traffic

    Commonly known as Facebook or Google ads, paid traffic is an effective way to drive larger numbers of your ideal clients into your sales funnel. These can work well because you can target your ideal clients, but there's a certain amount of skill needed to get them set up and optimised well.

Action 3: Utilise Facebook groups

6

When you consider that Facebook is one of the biggest marketing tools in the world, and it's free, you can quickly see why having a Facebook Group filled with the right people and the right positioning is a powerful strategy for your business.

Running a Facebook group isn't for everyone, and it depends on your ideal clients and how you like to show up in your business. If you do have one, you should talk about your group everywhere to grow it with organic traffic.

What actually makes a Facebook Group good? (And it does have to be good if you want people to stay.)

First, establish a clear reason for why you started the group and communicate it. Make sure people know what your group stands for, and they'll be much more likely to stay. Ultimately, they need to understand why you and why this group.

Have a strong name for your Facebook Group. It shouldn't be too long. Make it memorable so it hooks people in and they can remember it so they can search for it. People can easily forget the names of the groups they joined, and then won't be able to find them. If you can, let them see what they will get from joining by including the outcome in the title.

Be strict with who you let in because you need to have it filled with the right people. With my groups, I have a strict no-promo policy because I know with business groups this can be a big problem. There are people out there who just join groups to fish for clients, which can, unfortunately, dilute the mission and vision you have for the group.

At the same time, be personable and welcoming. Respond to questions and show your appreciation for people taking the time to engage with your posts. Always be friendly and positive. Your group should be a nice place for your members to hang out. This means no bad-mouthing or criticism, as people don't need that in their lives. Build that all-important know, like, and trust system.

Your Facebook Group is a place for people to be sociable, so encourage engagement, ask questions, and make connections. You can do this by asking plenty of questions to get people talking.

If a Facebook Group isn't for you, or it's not where your ideal clients would hang out, that's no problem. But think about what you can do instead.

Action 4: Create a freebie/opt-in/lead magnet

An essential part of building a pipeline of leads that flow into your business is creating a freebie, otherwise known as an opt-in or lead magnet.

The idea is to offer something of value in exchange for your ideal client's email address. Lead magnets play a huge part in driving leads to your business, and without a steady supply of client enquiries, you'll feel like you're forever chasing your next client, which is stressful and causes unpredictable income.

Lead magnets usually offer digital, downloadable content, such as a free PDF checklist, report, eBook, etc., and the valuable information you will receive in exchange is someone's email address. As a mechanism to generate leads and email subscribers, you can do this in many ways, not just with PDFs. You can send mini-email sequences, free workshops, videos or access to your online interviews. You can even start challenges your audience can follow.

Email addresses are valuable because it is a very personal medium. Even if someone on social media enjoys your brand, they are unlikely to just hand over their email address to you without a compelling reason. As an online business owner, it is your responsibility to persuade them.

6

The lead magnet itself is only half the equation – it's also about getting it in front of the right people and enough of them. The copy, title, and content are all important, but you can have the best lead magnet in the world and if no one sees it, then it might as well not exist.

Action 5: Master email marketing

Email marketing content is one of the best approaches to maintaining a personal and continuous relationship with your target market. As I explained in the last action, to succeed with email marketing, give something away for free in exchange for the consumer's email address, and it must be something of value.

If you have a visitor on your website who doesn't buy, the next best thing is to capture their email address. An easy and effective way to do that is to create a pop-up sign-up form on your website. This should ideally offer your audience something in exchange. The purpose is to develop a relationship with that consumer through drip-fed campaigns using automated systems.

However, don't try to constantly sell in your email marketing. This is about developing a strategy to succeed by focusing on relationship building. When it comes to building your subscriber list, there are three things to keep in mind:

1.   Welcome your target audience by sending them personalised emails that help them gain trust in

you. In this email, you should keep them interested by sharing useful content.

2. Nurture them through a series of emails that position you as the person to help them.

3. Once they hear enough to know, like, and trust you, it is time to invite them to commit and invest while also delivering content that will handle objections and empower them to make a decision. It's important you don't push them – your help and attitude should step them towards you.

Now you know how to increase your visibility, you can go a step further and nail down your social media strategies. We'll dive into this in the next chapter.

6

Key Points

- If you want to make repeatable sales in your business, you need a big enough pond to fish in. Building an audience isn't just about finding people to sell your products and services to. You have to also build a relationship with those people by demonstrating your position and credibility as a coach.
  - Action 1: Use fear as fuel to put yourself out there
  - Action 2: Build an audience organically first
  - Action 3: Utilise Facebook groups
  - Action 4: Create a freebie/opt-in/lead magnet
  - Action 5: Master email marketing

Step #7:
Craft a Winning Content Strategy

Social media is one of the quickest and most powerful ways of raising visibility. It allows us to connect to and have conversations with so many potential clients. Social media has transformed the landscape of running a business, so we should leverage the technology at our fingertips. Because so many people want to hear from you, and these channels are your routes straight to them.

Craft a Winning Content Strategy

For the first six months of her business, Lianne was posting on Instagram every day, but this wasn't translating into enquiries, let alone sales. She was getting increasingly disillusioned and wondering if she was cut out for building a coaching business.

Lianne and I worked together for 18 weeks in one of my programmes, and then she booked a half-day intensive with me to solidify her plan. Together, we built a way for Lianne to massively boost her visibility online and get noticed by more of the right people.

The marketing material she was writing was given an overhaul, so it spoke to her ideal clients and connected with what they were feeling. People buy with emotion, so this was an important step. She created resources that her ideal clients wanted and started to build an email list of people who needed what she had to offer. Finally, we also developed a clear strategy for how she could maximise her social media to offer more valuable content to her target audience.

7

This transformed her business resulting in more enquiries and sales, but more importantly, her confidence went through the roof. By focusing on increasing her visibility not only on her website but on social media, Lianne increased her pool of clients and built a strong revenue stream for her coaching business.

In the following sections of Step 7, I'll share more about the strategies that Lianne and I built for her business so you can also learn from them.

The 5 Actions to Crafting a Winning Content Strategy

While visibility is a crucial aspect of creating success in business, it isn't enough. Because content is still king. Our content as a business owner is the currency with which we attract our audience, engage with them, make them raving fans of our brand, and convert them to paying customers. And much of our content is now shared via social media.

Despite a lot of stigma around the effect of social media on mental health and that a large percentage of the population uses social media only for personal purposes, there are so many reasons why, as a business owner, you should be on social media and taking advantage of its power to connect you with hundreds or even thousands of your future clients.

A vast majority of your audience can be found on one (or many) of the social media platforms that exist today. If the effects of the COVID-19 pandemic have taught us anything,

7

it is that we must prepare our businesses to be scalable with or without a physical presence. It is only with tools such as social media, your website, or your blog that your business can keep afloat in a world going completely digital.

Action 1: Reframe your mindset around social media

Just like any venture you pursue, your ability to succeed with social media starts with your mindset and what you think and feel about what you are setting out to do. Our attitude and mindset are so critical that having a negative mindset or certain limiting beliefs towards social media can hold us back from successfully harnessing its true potential on any platform.

You may have picked up these limiting beliefs from what you heard about social media from others. Maybe they developed over time as you tried to use the platform and ended up frustrated, tired, or overwhelmed.

However, as you set out to become strategic about 'winning' on social media, we must first debunk and put away these limiting beliefs so you have an open mind towards growth and making significant progress with any social media platform.

The first of these limiting beliefs is thinking that you don't have anything valuable to say. Imposter syndrome can, at times, cripple our actions, and this is no different when it comes to social media. How often do you find yourself asking, "What would I even say?" or "Who would want to read this"?

The truth is that you have your knowledge and expertise. You have experience. You have stories to tell, struggles you have overcome (or not), things you have grown to love or dislike, habits that have shaped your life, and so much more that makes you, you.

The second limiting belief is thinking social media is not important for growing your business. With social media, we have the privilege of starting a business from scratch and building it to a point we are happy with. Not just with the money we make but with the influence we have on others and the impact we create in our field – this is growth.

The last most common limiting belief is doubting the effectiveness of social media because you are not seeing instant engagement. Vanity metrics such as likes and follows make us look down on our efforts and feel like the entire endeavour is not worth it. But the reality is that just because someone does not like or comment on your post does not mean they do not see it. Your clients are not just the people who like your posts or comment on them every day.

Social media is not a video game where you win or lose at the end of each round. It's a part of your business; it's a continuous venture where you should focus more on the journey and less on the finish line.

Action 2: Craft your brand guidelines around a deep understanding of your audience

The most successful business owners understand their audience in deep detail. When you truly understand your audience, it is much easier to paint a clear picture of where they are right now, emotionally and physically, where they want to get to, and what is needed to get there.

While it is not important to have every detail figured out, you should have an idea of the kind of people you want to work with at the very beginning. This is because as your business grows, you will need to refine your audience and tune 'what you think you know' to 'what the reality actually is'.

Start with what you know about your audience today by stepping right into their shoes and looking through their lens, not your own. This will help you create your unique brand guidelines to take your coaching business forward.

There are six elements to keep in mind when building your brand online:

7

- Brand name
  While it may not immediately seem like it matters, it is important your brand name reflects your identity and what you offer. This makes it much easier and quicker for potential clients to determine if they want to connect with you.

- Brand story

    Your audience needs an inspirational role model, and to know that you are the person who can solve their problem and create transformation for them or help them to create their own transformation.

- Brand values

    Your brand values are arguably the most essential element of your brand guideline. Why? Because your audience will only connect with or associate themselves with values that resonate with them, no matter how attractive your offer.

- Brand voice

    Your brand voice is simply what you would like to sound like on social media. Do you want to sound fun and exciting? Do you want to sound calm and soothing? How would you like to sound to your audience?

- Unique Selling Position

    One of the reasons we sometimes struggle to acquire clients is that we are not clear on our unique superpower. Why should your potential clients come to you rather than your competitors? How can you win me over if you pitch to me as a client?

- Brand channels

  One of the most commonly asked questions is: what social media platform(s) do I need to be on? And the answer is simple: the platform(s) where your target audience exists. However, if you are just starting or you handle your social media marketing yourself, it's important to stick to a maximum of 1 or 2 platforms to ensure you take full advantage of the potential of these platforms before moving on to others. This also defines what kind of content you need to create. If your brand channel is YouTube, you need to make more videos. If your channel is Instagram, you need a strong mix of images and videos, and so on.

Action 3: Define your content pillars and map out your content calendar

Content pillars are umbrella topics that represent the entirety of your social media presence. Your content pillars should centre on who you are, what your business does, and what you would like to talk about.

Usually, your content topics revolve around your core niche, focus, or industry. They should inform your social media strategy and enable you to build consistency in what you talk about and the content you create. For example, if

7

you are a wellness coach helping working-class mums through burnout and depression, your content pillars might include things like:

- Stigma around burnout and depression
- Overcoming burnout/depression
- Wellness of the mind/a wellness lifestyle
- Lifestyle practices that support healthy and wholesome living

To figure out your content pillars, think about your most significant area of expertise. What do you want your brand to be known for? What problems are you out to solve? And what can you provide the most information on based on your experience?

Once you figure out your content pillars, further divide them into themes to define the goal of your content. This may be to engage with your audience, educate them, or build a personal connection with followers. Every piece of content you create and every post you share should have an objective.

Identifying these themes will help you to build a cohesive content calendar. A content calendar is simply a mapped-out schedule of what you plan to post on your social media channel of choice for a given period.

Filling up your content calendar is easier than you think. You can use this formula to come up with content ideas:

1. What is your business goal for the month?
2. Select a content pillar that ties to this business goal
3. Select a content theme

4. Merge the content pillar and content theme to create your content item for the day
5. See what content you can repurpose. We're all about making things easy to remember!

Action 4: Grow your social media numbers and boost engagement

One of your business priorities should be to keep your numbers growing, and there are various ways to achieve this. The bigger the pond you have to fish in, the more people will be interested in your content and offers.

Let's look at three ways you can boost engagement and build more trust and communication between you and your audience while growing your numbers. These are video content, groups, and direct messaging.

•   Video Content
    By showing your face more or in real-time, you build trust with your audience and make them feel at ease to share themselves with you. Whether it's Instagram Live, reels, stories, feed posts, or others, video content gives off a friendly vibe that your audience will often reciprocate.

•   Groups
    These can be Facebook, WhatsApp, or

7

LinkedIn groups. Social media groups are a great way to build engagement with an online audience. This can be approached in two ways – you can decide to join a group or create one yourself. Whatever you decide, groups can be highly beneficial to your social media growth and to your audience conversion when properly optimized. I'd recommend you join 2–3 groups. Remember, these are spam-free zones. The idea isn't to pitch but to connect and grow your network.

- Direct Messaging

    Even though DMs have been given bad credit as social media bots and spam accounts emerge, they are still a great way to engage with your audience and prime them for your main offer. Some rules of DMs you want to stick to:

    - Send more DMs to people who follow you or who you follow
    - Do not start a DM conversation with a sales pitch
    - You do not need to send a DM to everyone who follows you. Ensure they meet the criteria for your target audience before messaging them.

- Use engagement tools (such as IG stories) and your feed posts to get your audience talking about a topic related to your niche and then follow up the conversation with a DM.

Action 5: Follow the rules of copywriting for social media

The words you use and how you communicate them can make or break your business. They are the interface between you and the people you'd love to work with – they do an important job. The psychology behind all copywriting is in one question your potential audience asks: "What's in it for me?"

Once you can clearly articulate what your potential client is getting from your offer, you are on an excellent path to selling. So how do you sell with your words?

First, understand the pain point of your potential client. What are they struggling with right now? What emotions are they feeling?

Next, understand their desire. What is their dream scenario? What do they want to achieve?

Finally, create a link between their struggles and their desired state to paint a clear picture of the transformation they seek (which ultimately is your offer). We also covered this process in the messaging exercise in Step 3.

7

All copywriting is unique and different for everyone, and it is important you do not imitate someone else's copy. It's also essential to keep in mind these copywriting rules when creating content that sells or promotes your offer:

- Speak directly to one person

    Using the second-person point of view is a fundamental copywriting rule. Through this, your writing takes on the form of a dialogue, giving the reader the sense of a back-and-forth conversation with you.

- Start with an attention-grabbing headline that stops them scrolling past

    Getting people to read the rest of your page, email, popup, or article depends heavily on how you frame the headline. Only two out of ten people will read the rest of your content after reading the headline.

- Lead with value/service

    Copywriting should always answer the reader's main question: "What's in it for me?" The words you post should offer something that the reader can use or will find valuable. This will also encourage them to relate to your brand and explore what services you offer.

- Engage with storytelling

  Despite being challenging to execute, storytelling is one of the most effective copywriting techniques. Stories excel at stirring up emotion and building connection.

- Get to the point

  No one likes reading a long piece of content. Especially now viewers' attention spans are getting shorter and shorter online. So, make sure your copy is clear and succinct so people won't skip reading it.

- Write in your audience's words

  Copywriting is knowing whom you're writing for. If your audience consists of corporate professionals looking for a mindset coach, what words and terms would resonate with them?

- Always review as a buyer

  When you have a piece of copy written, always review it before posting. Consider if it appeals to your buyer's persona and if the words resonate with what they find valuable.

7

Getting your social media strategy right will take time and hard work. But by following these five actions, you'll know exactly what to do and in what order. Remember, the point of using social media for your business isn't to get likes and followers. It's about using your content to get in front of the right people and converting them into clients.

The next step in the Signature Framework is learning how to sell confidently and enjoying it.

7

KEY POINTS

- Our content as a business owner is the currency with which we attract our audience, engage with them, and convert them to paying customers. As a business owner, you should be on social media to take advantage of its visibility.
  - Action 1: Reframe your mindset around social media
  - Action 2: Craft your brand guidelines around a deep understanding of your audience
  - Action 3: Define your content pillars and map out your content calendar
  - Action 4: Grow your social media numbers and boost engagement
  - Action 5: Follow the rules of copywriting for social media

7

Step #8:
Sell Confidently

An excellent way to shift your thinking on selling is to view it not as selling but as a way of supporting people. It's your way of connecting and serving clients. The money you receive is the byproduct of doing the work you love and helping people. If you learn to enjoy the process of serving clients and do it confidently, you'll have a huge impact on their lives. While also receiving the revenue that comes with this.

Sell Confidently

S ophie is a coach who works with people who want a career change. Her clients have reached a point where they think something is missing in their working life, and they want to explore the alternatives. Before Sophie and I started working together, she was having trouble getting to grips with the idea of selling. She loved helping people and transforming lives but had resistance to selling her programmes.

Sophie would book a call with a potential client, but during their conversation, she wouldn't know how to properly package her offer so that it spoke to that person's needs. She was doing two things that were causing a bigger problem in her business. She was either not selling at all, so missing the opportunity altogether, or trying to sell something she thought that person needed rather than what they *actually* needed, which led to a mismatch and ultimately no sale.

Once we recognised this problem, Sophie and I worked together to come up with a plan.

The key thing was to change her mindset about selling

8

and build her confidence to talk to people about her offers. We also worked on asking the right questions during discovery calls to properly understand what her clients were looking for. This way, she could give them what they wanted rather than what she thought they wanted, which will always lead to a more successful outcome.

Fast forward to today, and Sophie has packed programmes full of the right kind of people, and she's changing lives. She's also building a name for herself as the go-to coach in her niche. She has got clear on how to uncover what people are looking for so she could sell the solution.

Just like Sophie, you too can conquer the fear, confusion, and the feelings of being overwhelmed when it comes to selling, and this part of the Signature Framework will teach you the actions you need to achieve just that.

The 6 Actions to Selling Confidently

What are your thoughts on selling? Do you hate this part of your business? Perhaps you know you need to do it, but are uncomfortable talking about money with people.

Whatever your approach to selling, it is a skill you must develop to have a thriving business. Because without sales, it's not a business – it's a hobby. Selling is not an afterthought in your business. It's the beating heart of your business that will secure its longevity and help ensure your support for future clients, while providing for yourself and your family.

Sales also have to be treated ethically. There shouldn't be

8

any arm-twisting or backing anyone into a corner. This is for two reasons. Firstly, that isn't a particularly pleasant way to go about it. Secondly, if you have to force someone into buying from you, I can pretty much guarantee they won't be your ideal client, which might cause you problems down the line.

Instead, selling is all about what you can do for someone else. In the next section, we'll discuss what actions you can take to sell more confidently.

Action 1: Reframe your mindset around selling

If the idea of selling makes you squirm, you are not alone. Many of the people I work with find this part of running a business really difficult. Often, they love what they do and are amazing at it, but are much less enthusiastic about charging what it's worth and telling the world. Coaches and business owners often talk about how they are 'not good at selling.' It feels icky, and they just can't find the words to sell their services.

This fear of sales didn't start with the advent of online businesses, as people have always felt a certain way about sales. But have you ever thought about why that's the case? What is so bad about selling? After all, you want to run a successful business, which means making money from it.

The truth is, no one is born a naturally 'good' salesperson. It is a skill we all have to learn if we want to build a business that is truly successful and thriving. Adopting the right

8

mindset around selling is the first step:

If you have a product or service that can help someone…

If you have knowledge you can share that will make a difference to someone's life…

If you see people with a problem you know you have the solution for…

You owe it to these people to tell them about your solution.

This is true whether it is a product or service.

Therefore, shift your mindset from chasing potential clients to showcasing the information that will attract them to you.

If you show people how you can help solve their problems – and do it with confidence and conviction – they will pay you. And they'll do this with gratitude and ease, with no arm twisting required.

Action 2: Craft a sound sales plan

In business, we need to set goals around selling. A sales goal helps keep you accountable. Remember the saying about planning to fail when you fail to plan? It applies here as well. When you don't define your sales goals, you automatically set yourself up for no sales because there's nothing to work towards.

You need to set sales goals when launching new offers or filling out your programmes or events. There should be a number you want or need to reach. By consistently setting up your sales goals, you create a much easier system to track your marketing and promotional activities and keep tabs on what works and what doesn't.

You may already be familiar with the concept of S.M.A.R.T goals, but for those who aren't, your sales goals must be S.M.A.R.T – Specific, Measurable, Achievable, Relevant, and Time-bound.

Feel free to create your own version, but make sure you use the concepts properly when setting your targets. Let's look at each aspect more closely:

- Specific

    Rather than having a sales goal of 'Make £100,000 this year', detail how you will reach that goal by breaking it into months or quarters. If you are new to coaching or your business isn't yet firmly established, you might want to weight the higher revenue months towards the end of the year to give yourself a chance to build momentum at the beginning of the year. Alternatively, there might be campaigns you're running across specific months, so you will expect a higher revenue at these points during the year. Ultimately, you will need to break your annual revenue goal into smaller targets.

- Measurable

    This is about measuring your goals to know if

8

you're making progress. Looking at our previous example of 'Make £100,000 this year', how can you measure the true value of that goal? Is it £100,000 in profit or £100,000 in revenue? Or even £100,000 in future sales? And how will you track the numbers to know when you've reached this goal? Which offers will you sell to reach this figure? Where possible, make your goals quantifiable so you can check in and review your progress at any given time.

- Achievable

    How often have you thought to yourself something like, 'I have an email list of 2000 subscribers, so I'm going to launch this programme to them. And I'm hoping to get at least 100 clients'? Or... 'I'm hosting a free webinar, and I will get 500 attendants. So, at the end of that, I should enrol 20 new clients'?

    In a perfect world, these numbers are feasible and make sense. After all, a general rule of thumb in sales is to place your conversion rate between 2% and 10%. But if you have an audience that isn't primed to your offer (i.e. they're not completely aware of what it is you do or who you are), you may want to set your sales goal at a 2% conversion. This means your email list of 2000 contacts will convert

40 people, or your webinar with 500 attendants will convert 10 people.

While these may seem like low numbers, it's important to set stretching goals but be realistic based on probable industry benchmarks.

- Relevant

  The reality is we often forget what is relevant to our business or get distracted by 'shiny objects'. When you set your sales goals, first review them and ask, is this relevant to my business as a whole? Remember your sales goals should come from business goals, not vice versa.

- Time-bound

  Your sales goals should have an end date. Setting a deadline focuses your mind and makes it more likely you'll achieve the desired results. You might want to establish monthly, bi-monthly, or even quarterly sales goals. But you shouldn't have an endless goal you are constantly trying to catch up with.

8

Action 3: Know when to upsell and downsell

Upselling and downselling are further sales routes you can direct your clients to. You either upsell them into a more expensive offer or downsell them into a cheaper one. A great way to create upselling and downselling strategies is through your sales funnel. As we covered in Step 5, a sales funnel is a 'top-down' process in which leads or potential customers are guided through different automated points of contact and content, which ultimately leads to a sale for your business. When you set up funnels, you create additional ways for your business to make money without actively 'selling' because funnels emulate your sales process but run on autopilot. You set them up once and continuously reap the benefits.

Let's look at how upselling and downselling could work with a group coaching programme. If your programme costs £500 per client and you can only handle ten clients per month, you are limited to £5,000 in revenue each month. Even if you attract more leads at the bottom of your funnel, you will have reached capacity.

But what happens if you incorporate upsells and downsells in your sales funnel?

Say a potential customer visits your website or sales page and spends £500 on an online course. After making that purchase, or during the purchasing process, you could present them with an upsell product. This would be a related product that would help them to get a bigger, better, faster result. Something that would sit nicely alongside the thing

8

they've just bought.

Now, there's every chance the customer might decline this upsell or order bump, but there's still the possibility that they might add it to their purchase, and if they do, you'll make more money from this transaction. This is an upsell or order bump.

Let's say a customer comes to the same online course, but instead of hitting the button to buy and spending £500, they leave the page. Perhaps they've enrolled for an event you're running and have decided that even though the event has been helpful, it's not the right time for them. This doesn't mean that any selling opportunity has disappeared, far from it. It simply means you're presenting them with an offer they don't want to buy, and the chances are if you present them with an offer that is a better fit, they will buy.

So, instead of offering your online course, you could offer a lower-priced option that gets them stepping forward and making some progress, ultimately moving them closer towards the higher ticket item you may sell them further down the line.

You can see from this example how effective upselling and downselling are for raising both your profits and the total lifetime value of your customers. This means you could make much more than the original £5,000 each month, which was capped. Therefore, upselling and downselling can double or possibly triple your sales when used strategically.

You can still offer the upsells and downsells without auto-mation and simply introduce them into conversations. But the funnel makes it easier as it does the heavy lifting for you.

8

Now, let's talk about when and how to upsell and down-sell as there are a few rules of thumb that applies to both:

- Ensure your upsells and downsells are relevant to your offer. You don't want to sell an e-book or course on food plans and diets if you are a business coach.
- Simplify rather than complicate. Don't get caught up in 'fluff'.
- Include ethical urgency and scarcity. These sales strategies help give your potential client a much-needed boost and get them to make the buying decision. You can add a countdown timer, a 48-hour discount, offer limited-time free calls, etc. Make sure they are ethical though. In other words, don't say there are only five if this isn't the case.

Action 4: Overcome objections with comfort

Handling a 'no' is one of the most uncomfortable yet important aspects of any sales call. Instead of it signalling the end of the conversation, it's better to think about the no differently. Because no doesn't always mean no. It might mean:

- Not now
- I'm not sure
- I need more information
- There's something I haven't understood
- I don't see the value

A sales objection isn't always a potential client rejecting your offer but possibly a fear or reservation you need to address. Objections are not a bad thing, they help you understand how your future client feels about your offer and provide opportunities to strengthen that initial bond between you and them.

Here are a few points to note when it comes to handling sales objections:

1. There are genuine reasons why someone may not be able to make a purchase immediately

    These often relate to time and money. As a business owner, approach each person from a place of empathy and understanding. If they genuinely cannot take you up on your offer now, perhaps schedule time in the future to reconnect. This is never about arm twisting.

2. Identify false objections

    Many potential buyers give false objections due to their fear or distrust. This is perfectly normal and allows you to gracefully let them know you understand their viewpoint while showing the value of your offer.

3. Give examples of clients/case studies where necessary

    Share examples of someone else who had a similar concern and how the previous client

8

trusted you and the benefits they acquired as a result.

4.   Always keep the conversation positive
     Maintain high levels of respect and positivity throughout your sales call – even when handling objections. Never use tactics that make the person you're speaking to feel uncomfortable or forced into a corner.

Remember, building trust is essential as people need reassurance from you that it's the right step for them. It's important you approach this with your client at the centre. This is about them, not you. You're likely to be speaking to them because they have a problem they want to fix, and it might be that they can't fix it unless they take a step forward.

Action 5: Realise the power of storytelling

Done well, storytelling builds connection and trust and can lead to phenomenal business growth because people feel connected with you. Your stories resonate, and they feel you're both on the same page.

8   When we tell stories, be they inspiring, educational, or just funny ones from our everyday life, we invite our audience, our listeners, to see our true selves. We are showing who we really are behind the camera, the social platforms and the glamour of the online world. But besides sharing

random stories of ourselves with our community, there is one story we must identify, define, and share as our ultimate truth – our hero's story.

Why is it important to have a hero's story?

Well, first, there is a reason you want people to pick you over others in your niche or industry. There is something that makes you different, something unique about you that places you as the right person for them. Everyone wants the very best for themselves, and this applies to services and coaches too.

Secondly, we mustn't assume our clients know why they want to work with us, so we must clearly articulate our unique point of difference. We should share the experiences we've been through that make us the best possible fit for our client. Remember, people don't buy coaching – they buy coaches. They also buy what they understand.

Of course, anyone can promise to help you 'live your best life' or 'make 5 or 6 figures in business'. Whether these claims are true is a different conversation.

Think about your own core promise. Now consider how you can clearly articulate your story in a way that is authentic and resonates with your audience and prospective clients. When sharing your story, whether that's why you started your business or what drives you, there's a way to do it well. Your story needs structure and purpose.

Consider these three elements:
1.   What were things like before?
2.   What was the catalyst for change?
3.   What is life like now, after the change?

8

Show them how this helps others and what you want them to do next, and remember:

- Keep your story concise
- Think in specific moments
- Connect the listener with feelings and emotion
- Talk about the details and nuances that make it compelling
- Be vulnerable but share the scar, not the wound.
- It's not about what's raw and emotional for you – it's about the lessons that come later.
- Always talk about the lesson because this connects your story to the person hearing it.

Action 6: Master winning sales calls

For most coaches, the route to more clients lies in discovery calls, which are, of course, really sales calls. Your sales call or discovery call should follow a process if you want to achieve the best results.

It should raise your future clients' awareness of their situation, connect them with their vision of success and demonstrate powerfully that you're the person to support them to achieve this. Here are the five elements to consider when structuring your sales call. Following this framework should lead to more of your ideal clients being ready to sign up.

8

1. Emotion

    What's the problem? How is this affecting their life? What's the consequence? What are they putting up with? How bad is it? Who else is it affecting? What if they don't fix it?

    This action is about connecting you and your client with the emotion behind their situation. Without raising their awareness of the emotion, they won't take positive steps. People buy with their emotional brain instead of their logical brain, so this action is crucial.

2. Vision

    Make their vision for the future big. When do they want to achieve it, and what difference will it make? Who else will benefit? How will they feel, and what will they be able to do that they can't now? Is this a now or later goal?

3. Connection

    Show them you have listened by summarising or paraphrasing what they have told you, 'What you've told me is…' They need to believe you can help, and they need to know you understand. This builds trust, and trust is essential.

    8

4. Position

    Position yourself as the person who can help

them create the result they want. Talk about case studies and similar results you've helped others achieve. Tell them it's possible for them, too. Talk about your skills, expertise, credibility and why you're the person to best support them.

5. Solution

If you've done a good job and the call has gone well, it's possible they will ask you for the price and are ready to move ahead. If they're a good fit and you think you can help, tell them you can help them to achieve the results they want.

Ask permission to share how this could work or what it would look like. Offer a single option only because you already know what they need if you've asked the right questions and have a clear understanding of their next steps. When you offer multiple options, people get confused about which one they should take and invariably end up taking none.

Talk about the top-level structure to avoid overwhelming them. Don't pile on information. Instead, give them a high-level view. They don't need the detail. They need to know you can help them reach the desired outcome.

8

Tell them what will happen first. You can say something like, 'When you sign up, the first thing you'll receive is a welcome pack, and we'll get your first 1:1 session booked in.' Give them something positive and exciting to look ahead to. Then, talk about results, 'This will support you in building/doing/creating/having, and I'll support you every step of the way.'

Move the conversation forward with one of the following questions:

'Does that sound like something that would support you?'

'Would you like to know the investment?'

After that, you could offer two payment options, one in full and a payment plan. The payment plan should be higher as you're taking the risk of them not making all the payments and there is also additional administrative work of processing more payments. Also, rewarding people who pay in full is a nice touch. Always lead with the payment plan, then offer the discount for paying in full rather than a perceived penalty for paying in instalments. Finally, thank them for coming on the call with you and clearly explain the next steps.

8

Learn how to launch successfully

As we mentioned earlier in this chapter, a big part of selling confidently is clarity on what you offer and how you'll get your target customers to buy. So, in addition to embracing the selling process, learn the art of creating a successful launch. This is so important it requires its own bonus section, because if potential clients aren't aware of your programme or course then they can't begin the process of considering whether to buy it.

In the world of marketing, a 'launch' is introducing your offer to the public. It's that time in your business when you show off your labour of love and officially promote and sell it. It's about making a splash about what's coming soon.

A launch can be as complex as a month-long series of events, including seminars, speakers, workshops, or open houses. Or it can be as simple as a sales page or an email saying, 'We're live!'

When you're confident in your ability to sell, the launch process can be made much easier. But before you get caught up in the hustle and bustle of the launch, you need to do your homework and build a solid offer. Some questions to ask yourself are:

- What exactly is your offer?
- What problem does it solve?
- Who does it solve a problem for?
- What are your emotional selling points?
- What is your overall customer promise?

In answering these questions, you validate your offer and

8

your launch.

Much like mastering a winning sales call, a successful launch also involves speaking to prospective clients. Find out what pain point they're currently facing. What is their desired transformation? And how can your offer bridge that gap?

A successful launch is delicate, it requires our time, effort, and in most cases, money. This is why we must be absolutely dedicated to its success. Setting your launch game plan can help you stay on track with your sales and goals. These are the elements that should make up your launch plan:

1. Launch goals

    Like crafting your sales plan, you need to set goals for your launch – Specific, Measurable, Achievable, Relevant, and Time-bound. Here's an example:

    Let's say you have an email list of 1000 sub-scribers and a social media audience of 2000 followers. You have decided your launch plan isn't going to involve paid ads, so your sales traffic will be organic.

    A good rule of thumb is to expect a 2–10% conversion rate if you are launching to a cold or somewhat warm audience. With these numbers in mind, is it feasible to set a launch goal of 300 purchases? Obviously not. In a best-case scenario, you may be able to land a whopping 150 purchases (5% of 3000).

8

Setting launch goals like this helps you manage your expectations and have a target to aim for.

2.   Your launch audience

It is vital that you work out who you are launching to. In most cases, you would have already built an audience, such as a Facebook group, email list, or social media community. Remember your offer defines your launch audience. Whether you're launching a digital course, membership, or group coaching programme, your target audience should be a group who will find your product or service attractive.

3.   Timelines and important dates

What is your launch timeline? The important dates you need to take note of include the following:

- Pre-launch start date: When do you intend to kick off pre-launch activities?
- Launch date: What is the official date of the launch?
- Launch end date: When is the cart-close date?
- Post-launch period: How long will you keep the cart open after

the launch has ended? This usually ranges from 24 hours to 1 week.

4.   Paid or organic traffic

Paid traffic for your launch includes tactics such as running social media ads, influencer marketing, or any marketing strategy that involves paying for an influx of potential customers.

On the other hand, organic traffic does not involve payment. Instead, you focus on your existing audience, such as your email list, social media followers, or subscribers. Organic traffic also involves anyone who stumbles on your page or website.

Both of these methods work well for launches, and neither is better than the other. The final decision lies with you in making the choice for your audience acquisition. Of course, you will want to consider things like cost, length of the launch period, expertise, current audience size, etc. before you reach the final verdict.

8

5.   Content plan

In alignment with your choice of audience, map out your content plan for the launch period. This should include what you post on your channels during the launch period. Your launch channels include email content, social media content, and other materials. If you are launching to an email list, you might want to send three emails per week for the period of your launch. If you are launching to your social media audience, you may want to create one feed post for Instagram and Facebook and one reel for Instagram.

6. Team and activities

Whether you have a dedicated team, an outsourced team or are a solopreneur, map out all the launch tasks for each team member. If you have a team, it's easier to dedicate launch tasks based on each member's role. If you are a solopreneur, you may still want to consider automating specific tasks such as content scheduling. Otherwise, you will have to handle everything yourself.

7. Map out your customer launch journey

List the step-by-step process you want your prospective clients to go through until they reach your offer. Here is an example of a typical customer journey for a course launch:

First, your prospective client will see your ad on Facebook or social media and click on it. Then, they'll be redirected to your freebie landing page, where they'll download your content. This adds them to your email list. After that, your prospect will receive your launch email series, where they'll click on the link in the email. Finally, they'll be redirected to the sales page, where they'll click 'Buy Now' and make payment.

8.   Pre-launch activities

The pre-launch phase is arguably the most important part. Pre-launch activities are the activities that lead to or introduce your launch. They prompt your audience to:

- Think more about the problem your offer solves
- Question the solution your offer provides
- Know, like, and trust you

Your pre-launch phase should be much longer than the launch period. A good pre-launch should be between three weeks to three months before your launch date. This gives you enough time to prep your audience for the launch and gain useful feedback.

Examples of pre-launch activities include weekly webinars and live sessions. It could also be going live on social media three times a week to ask questions about your offer. You

8

can also promote a freebie related to your offer.

9. Launch activities

Launch activities are the activities that make up your launch. Your launch phase is the official 'come and buy my offer' season. And if you've done your pre-launch well, you should already have a few clients at the door.

A common mistake entrepreneurs make is spending all their creative juices on the pre-launch. Then, when it's time for the launch, they sound like a broken record repeating the same thing over and over. Remember, the goal of your pre-launch is to build traction and validate your offer. Your launch, however, is all about selling. This is where you'll apply your new and improved confidence around sales.

10. Post-launch activities

Every good launch needs an 'extended cart open' period, for last-minute buyers. The post-launch phase is a delicate and flexible period to achieve two things:

- Do a final cart call

Sometimes, people just need that extra reminder or a final follow-up. This is also a great time to offer a limited-time discount, payment plan, or extra bonus. Again, gracefully introduce urgency and scarcity, reemphasising the value of your offer and the cost of their indecision.

- Gather feedback and measure the success of your launch

    More than anything, this should be a period of pure honesty and empathy with yourself. What went wrong? What went well? Did you meet your launch goals? What did your audience act on? What didn't they respond to? A helpful idea is to reach out to your launch audience directly, preferably by email, and ask why they didn't take action. This is not the time to be hard on yourself, whatever your launch results. If you map out a launch plan strategically and stick to it, you're going to see the results. And with each launch, the results get better and better.

Learning how to sell successfully will transform your coaching business into one where you never have a shortage of clients. Serving these clients to the best of your abilities and increasing your capacity will require systems to support you and make your business run like clockwork, which is what we will cover in the final step.

8

KEY POINTS

- You must develop selling skills to have a thriving business. Sales are the beating heart of your business that will secure its longevity and ensure your support for future clients, while providing for you and your family.
  - Action 1: Reframe your mindset around selling
  - Action 2: Craft a sound sales plan
  - Action 3: Know when to upsell and downsell
  - Action 4: Overcome objections with comfort
  - Action 5: Realise the power of storytelling
  - Action 6: Master winning sales calls

Step #9:

Implement Systems that Make Your Business Run Like Clockwork

When you do all the heavy lifting yourself in your business, things will fall between the cracks, opportunities will be missed, and your business might feel clunky and chaotic. As your business grows, it's vital to have the right systems and people around you so you can focus on your genius zone and minimise becoming overwhelmed. If you want to reach high revenue months and build a multi-dimensional business, you need automated systems and support.

Implement Systems That Make Your Business Run Like Clockwork

When my client, Bianca, started her coaching business, she immediately felt overwhelmed. Something she hadn't considered when transitioning from her full-time job to running her own business was that there was no one to tell her what her business should be like. She struggled finding clarity and focusing on what she wanted to create. Bianca had the freedom to decide how to run her company, but this freedom ended up being too much for her. She had so many ideas she wanted to implement, but they were jumbled in her mind. Bianca was busy every single day but not making much progress.

When Bianca and I finally had the opportunity to talk about her business, we devised a plan to help her create systems to support her in running her coaching business – from the initial stages of looking for clients all the way to growing and expanding her services. More importantly, I helped Bianca realise an important lesson: she didn't need to do everything in her business, especially when it left her with zero capacity for anything else.

After all the work, Bianca has reached a point where she has built a solid foundation that will allow her to level up. She put workflows and systems in place that eliminated the mess and overwhelmed feelings in her mind. Her business now works like clockwork, and she has the freedom to think creatively about where she wants to take it next.

One thing Bianca had to discard was the mindset that working harder brings more results – because it doesn't. Working smarter brings more results, which this chapter will cover. It will show you how to work smarter to get ahead faster without having to work long hours at the expense of seeing your kids or having to work while you're on holiday, which is the reality for a lot of coaches.

In the coaching world, a huge emphasis can be placed on the 'hustle' mentality. I'm at the opposite end of that spectrum. My approach is an anti-hustle 'less is more' and 'scaling simply' one. It's about stepping back from what you are doing, looking at what is slowing you down and improving it.

You can do this too. In this final step, we'll dive into the key elements that can help you remove the feeling of being overwhelmed and the tasks that unnecessarily take up your time so that you can focus on what you really want to be doing.

4 Actions to Establishing a Business That Runs Like Clockwork

There are several ways to systemise and create a business that runs like clockwork. The first part to this is realising you don't have to be the person doing everything within your company. If you are that person, it will be like driving down the motorway with the handbrake on. It will feel very slow, very overwhelming, and you won't get very far.

At the core of all productivity are the delegation and simplified systems that enable us to run our businesses as the CEOs we have decided to be. To do this, we develop a setup that ultimately leads to more money, time, and energy. Having this in place allows us to thrive and build a sustainable business that will stand the test of time.

There are a few ways you can leverage your time and get more done so that you can focus on your zone of excellence, which is coaching your clients and being the show-pony in your business. We need to manage our time well if we want to use our hours to the best of our abilities. You will need to be intentional about how you use your time, or the days will just run away with you.

We must always be the show-pony in our business and focus on the activities that only we can do. These are typically ones that generate revenue, build relationships and require our input.

When we focus instead on being the work-horse, we get caught up in the less essential daily tasks that are slowing us down. We get caught in the weeds.

9

The work-horse tasks can be outsourced or automated.

The show-pony activities need you and no one else.

Too many coaches get trapped into being work-horses. As a result, they get caught up in the everyday tasks of the business instead of focusing on generating bigger-picture results.

So, ask yourself: Am I the show-pony or the work-horse in my business?

If you think you're still being a work-horse, the next section of this chapter will reveal four actions to establish a business that runs like clockwork, allowing you to transition into being the show-pony you need to be.

Action 1: Define your processes

Before we can change how we do things, we need to know what our current processes are. One of the greatest achievements of the 21st century is that we no longer have to trade our time for money but can put workflows in place that make money without us actively being present. As well as helping our finances, workflows allow us to run our business without being the one doing everything and being everywhere.

One of the ways I've streamlined my time is by creating workflows for many of my processes. I did this by sitting down and looking at everything I was doing. I mapped out my regular activities and broke everything down into the individual steps because I knew this would help me with five

key things:
- It would save me time
- It would make my activities easily repeatable
- It would give my clients a better experience
- It would make outsourcing far easier
- It would show me what I could automate

My favourite way to do this was by listing the individual steps in a dedicated board called 'workflows'. I mapped out workflows for everything: onboarding and offboarding clients, creating content, email marketing, monthly reviews, and building funnels. Once it was clearly laid out in front of me, I knew exactly what was involved in running my business.

I ended up with a board jam-packed with step-by-step processes. It was incredibly powerful and meant when my team expanded, I had something to hand over to them to introduce them to my business.

As well as defining my processes, it highlighted the gaps where I could be generating further income. Below are examples of additional steps you can add to workflows to build in more recurring revenue for your business:
- Set up an upsell or downsell for a course, e-book, or product immediately after a purchase.
- Reference these inside your course and include a link to make a purchase.
- Partner with complimentary course creators and include an affiliate link at the end of the course.
- Set up a partner programme for your course and

9

invite past students to become partners.

- Set up a membership subscription, as this encourages recurring revenue.
- Include gift cards or coupons.
- Cross-sell similar or complementary products.
- Host virtual events and sell the replay as one-off products.
- Add links to upsell your past students into a membership or mastermind.
- Create an email sequence that transitions from a free download to a low-cost downloadable.

Defining processes is something I do with all my clients when we begin working together as well. Together, we map out how customers move through their business, whether coming in through a lead magnet, as a paying customer or attending one of their events.

This work is essential as you won't know whether you need to hire people or what areas can be automated until you are clear on the exact processes in your business.

Action 2: Automate

Once you know your processes, automate as many as possible. The next steps of a workflow process will then be generated without your input. The less time you spend on these essential but minor tasks, the more time you can spend on the show-pony work that only you can fulfil.

9

Automation also allows for growth because, without automated systems, you will reach the cap of how much you can fit into a day. Once you meet that point, you must choose between working longer hours or turning clients away.

Many of my clients initially believe that automation is boring, but they soon change their minds when it generates tens of thousands a month. This is because automation isn't just about tidying up your email auto-responses. When done properly, it makes sales for you. Whether you're selling programmes, online courses or retreats, you have to get those offers in front of enough people. Automating and sys-temising gives you a massive step up because you don't have to be personally involved in the marketing and sales. They happen in the background, allowing you to be the show-pony in the foreground.

The last chapter was about selling confidently because sales are the bare bones of your business, and people won't want to buy from someone who isn't confident in their own services. But often, coaches need additional help, and auto-mation takes the burden of the sales being solely on your shoulders, particularly if it's not your forte.

After years of working with coaches, most I encounter are not naturals at marketing or selling. This is because most coaches I meet are qualified, trained coaches who have gone into business because they are passionate about helping people and transforming lives. They're coming into coach-ing from an altruistic lens.

Whereas on the other side of the coaching space are

9

people who are coaches in a much looser sense of the word. They make promises such as six figures in six weeks and come into coaching from a business lens rather than a pure coaching approach.

Whether or not you are great at sales, marketing systems and automation are the secret weapon of every successful coach. When I was thinking about this for my business, I created CoachSpace.ai, along with my husband. I had used the same business management platform for years but was struggling with scaling my business. It didn't have everything I needed in one place, and I relied on too many different tech systems. I knew the best way to automate systems is to have one business management platform that holds every task.

One platform is the optimal way rather than scattered tech solutions because you don't have to worry about different systems connecting. Whenever you integrate two systems, it creates a weak spot where something can go wrong. It also usually works out cheaper if you're paying for one subscription that takes care of everything rather than for 3–10 separate services.

With my business partners, we mapped out all the steps coaches take clients on and, with this information, created a high-powered tech platform. Our aim was to help coaches create more impact and make more money by automating and simplifying their sales and marketing processes so they free up their time and focus on the right things. While the coaches do that, emails and social media posts will be sent out to draw potential clients into their funnels.

Some people say that automations are unglamorous. Do you know what's more unglamorous than building automations? Having to hustle hard for every sale.

Action 3: Outsource where necessary

When you struggle to do everything yourself, you mostly end up doing nothing. Outsourcing is the term used for hiring freelancers outside your business to perform services on your behalf.

When I started my coaching business, I hired a Virtual Assistant (VA) early on. I wasn't sure what I needed a VA for at that point, but I knew I wanted to go fast and having another pair of hands would help. Many coaches don't think they need a VA, but once you hire one, you will somehow miraculously manage to fill their time. It speeds up and creates momentum in your business.

I eventually realised I could automate some of the work my VA did. This realisation enabled me to get to the next level of growth. I could target my VA's time towards tasks that required the human element and leave everything else for automation. This improves efficiency, saves money and removes the element of human error.

If you want to work smarter, instead of thinking, 'What can I outsource?', begin with 'What can I automate?' Then, outsource what is left.

Of course, not everyone needs to outsource something in their business to a third party. You may just be starting in

9

your business, and perhaps you can't afford to outsource work right now. That's perfectly fine. You will know you're ready to outsource when:

1. You're making a decent amount of money in your business.
2. You can afford to pay someone a fraction of what you're making without running at a loss.
3. You're overwhelmed with work that pays really well. (If you're overwhelmed with work that doesn't pay, you have a pricing problem.)
4. You're mentally ready to let go of control over aspects of your business.
5. You have identified the areas you want to outsource and the tasks that can't be automated, which a third party would perform for you.

As your business grows, your team may also increase, and you might have a VA, a Tech VA and an Operations Manager, for example.

There is another side to why outsourcing or hiring a team is essential when you can afford it. There may be things you're not good at or cannot complete quickly. So, if you're not skilled at writing sales pages, you shouldn't be writing your sales page as it's important to get right. Equally, if it will take you a week, you should consider paying someone £300 to have it finished in two days. You can then free up your time to make more sales, look after your current clients or think about your next steps.

Consider what you're not doing in your business. What is

on your wish list you desperately want to do but never have the time for? So many business owners have things on their wish list they want to be doing and know will scale and grow their business, but still haven't got around to because they're too busy.

This is where defining your systems, automation, and outsourcing will help coaches free their time to take these leaps and create more impact on the world.

Action 4: Embrace AI

The next level up from defining your systems, automation and outsourcing is embracing AI.

We are in a new era of coaching where tech and AI are powerful dual systems. Some coaches have begun to use AI to create blogs or social media posts, but the power of AI goes way beyond that, and this is where we will be taking CoachSpace.ai. Harnessing AI technology offers various tools, from automation, virtual assistants and running your inbox to chatbots, analytics and more.

Leveraging AI is the future of business, and we need to think about whether we want to take that pioneering step forward. These tools are here to help us, and they're not going anywhere. The innovators who adopt AI are the ones who will push the boundaries of what is possible for a business.

If you look at the things that slow coaches down and what they find hard, it usually comes down to time. Coaches have

9

to wear many hats, and eventually, they hit a brick wall with how much time they have available. This is when it can step over from giving up your nine-to-five to swapping it for 24/7. The way I think about AI is that it helps do the things you don't want to do or are slowing you down.

AI could even mean you don't have to hire a team. You could get really smart and strategic about the tools and tech you're using to help your business run like clockwork so you can be the Queen Bee. In the past, coaches hired big teams. It was the case that the more successful your business, the more team members you had. I believe that the fewer team members you have, the more successful your business. I now run a lean operation. A year ago, I had seven team members, now I only have four.

The future of coaching is a combination of the human touch and technology. It will mean higher levels of efficiency for lower costs. Decades ago, we wore a badge of honour for working the longest, most demanding hours. That mentality is no longer fit for purpose. It doesn't serve us or those we care about, but ditching it doesn't mean we have to accept a dip in our success, either. Because there really is no limit to what you can achieve in your business if you've got the right tech and tools at your fingertips.

Fundamentally, the basis of coaching is relationships and helping people, and I don't believe that will ever change. As coaches, we are at our best when we are in front of our clients, helping them achieve huge transformations in their lives, whether in their relationships, health, careers or businesses. If that is what lights you up, if that is why you look

9

forward to starting work each day, then the answer is simple: aim to do more of that. Free up your time so you can do more of what you excel at, and the thriving, impactful coaching business you have always dreamed of will be within reach.

Now that we have covered the nine-step Signature Framework to creating your ideal coaching business, there is one final thing to cover: the final stretch to becoming the coach you *really* want to be.

Key Points

- The first step to creating a business that runs like clockwork is realising you don't have to be the person doing everything within your company. At the core of all productivity are delegation and simplified systems. These allow us to leverage our time and get more done so that we can focus on our zone of excellence, which is coaching our clients and being the show-pony, rather than the work-horse in our business.
  - Action 1: Define your processes
  - Action 2: Automate
  - Action 3: Outsource where necessary
  - Action 4: Embrace AI

The Final Stretch to Becoming the Coach You Really Want to Be

There's one final stretch to becoming the coach you really want to be. Maybe you've read this book over a couple of weeks, or you might have finished it in a day. Either way, you will struggle to become the remarkable coach you want to be unless these nine steps are *implemented*.

Without implementing all the actions contained within the steps, this book will just be a window into what could have been.

We have covered the essential advice and what the most innovative coaches are doing, but this information only matters if you go ahead and act. What really matters is what happens next.

The implementation process is naturally hard and is what people often need help with. This is why people work with coaches because they can't implement on their own as they need accountability and motivation.

The very best thing I can do for you now, the gift I can give you, is to help you implement what I've shared. Because

without action, without change, this book won't help transform your life. It's a waste of your time and mine, as I would
have written this book without fulfilling its purpose.

While my life and business look like a dream scene now,
how I got here isn't any different from your story. I didn't
achieve success or build my coaching business overnight. In
fact, navigating the roller coaster ride of entrepreneurship
sometimes seemed impossible.

I knew where I wanted to go, but I didn't know what I had
to do to get there quickly…until I got real with myself.

I recognised the problem that I didn't know what I didn't
know. I learnt what I needed to do and took action to
change my situation.

To tackle implementing these steps, let's recap the key
points in one place so you have them to hand at your desk.
You'll find them at the back of the book as a reference, just
flick to the last pages to find this handy guide. Then, you can
dive deep into the steps when you need more guidance.

The steps are designed to be tackled in order, but all nine
should be reviewed and tweaked throughout the year
because as your business grows, your approach to the different steps will too.

All nine must be in play because they are all equally
important and support each other. If you spend all your
time focusing on just one, your business won't take the giant
leap it could. If you focus on social media but haven't
defined your brand pillars, you will produce a lot of content
that doesn't resonate with your ideal client. Or if you concentrate on selling confidently but don't have irresistible

offers in place, it will impact the sales you can make.

The second way I will help you with implementation, accountability and motivation, is to send you a weekly reminder for twelve months so you can take forward each action and learn the review systems you need in place.

Think about where your business could be in a year's time if these essential parts were in play.

What would your work day look like?

How much money would you be making?

What would you do with your free time?

If you would like to take that first step of making a change in your business and receive these reminders, sign up at https://www.karenkissanecoaching.com/reminders. There is also a handy QR code on the next page.

Building your business is where hard work, self-belief, determination and perseverance are needed. I'm here to support you with all of these, just like I've helped thousands of people realise their fullest potential. I hope you join them in their successes and become the remarkable coach you deserve to be.

Work with Karen Kissane

If you're interested in learning more, don't hesitate to reach out to me after you've finished reading this book.

My website www.karenkissanecoaching.com has many free resources to help you grow and scale your coaching or service-based business.

There are also details of my paid programmes, including Breakthrough®, my online course, Thrive, my group programme, and various ways to work more closely with me in person or online, at retreats or in-person events.

I hope to see you soon!

Karen Kissane

Don't forget the weekly reminders to help implement all the steps in *The Remarkable Coach*:

Acknowledgments

To my family, Ivan, Ewan, and Imogen,

You might have thought *The Remarkable Coach* was just my secret code for "I'm hiding in my office with chocolate." For longer than I care to admit, you've heard me promise a book was on its way, yet you've seen more UFOs than evidence of this book's existence. Well, the moment has finally arrived, and it's got pages and everything! Thank you for your patience and for pretending to believe the book was more than just my imaginary friend. Ivan, I appreciate you more than you know as you've become a pro at juggling kids, business, life and catching me – often.

Thank you, Ewan and Imogen, for your casual acceptance of 'Mummy is writing a book' as if it's nothing out of the ordinary. This attitude might inspire you to become authors yourselves someday. I hope the incredible entrepreneurial life we lead, brimming with family board meetings at the dinner table and the life choices it brings us, inspires you to be more and have more.

And immense gratitude to my parents for always asking "How's the book coming along?" My dad for his expert eye on my book cover designs, and my mum for being excited about the launch party! I'm the first person in our family to have run a business, and I know there have been times (probably in equal measures) when you've flip-flopped between "We're so proud" to "Why on earth would you want to do this?"

To my extraordinary clients,

You are the stars of this book. Your trust, dedication, and willingness to embark on this amazing coaching adventure with me have inspired every word. Your journeys have shaped the pages, and your success stories are the gems within. Without these, *The Remarkable Coach* would be nothing but empty pages. Thank you for allowing me to be a part of your journey and for the privilege of sharing your successes with the world.

To my book coach, Amy,

You turned my chaotic jumble of words into a coherent and, dare I say, remarkable book. Your guidance, patience, and expert eye for detail turned this project into a reality. Thank you for believing in my vision and for polishing it into a shining gem. And the fact you were once my client and now I'm yours makes my heart sing. It's like we've swapped coaching capes, and I couldn't be more honoured to have your support. A true expert.

To my fantastic team,

You've seen it all – the late-night emails, the coffee over-dose, and the occasional incoherent rambling Slack message. You believed in this book when I was one coffee cup away from believing in unicorns. Your dedication and expertise have brought order to the chaos, and I can't thank you enough for being there.

To The Coaching Academy,

You were the spark that ignited this coaching journey. Thank you for introducing me to this world of coaching, where lives are transformed. Without any question, discovering this back in 2015 has changed my life as well as the lives of hundreds, if not thousands, of my clients and networks. A sliding doors moment that's created untold opportunities in my life as a direct result of coming to your free event.

Through The Coaching Academy, I also met Kris Robertson, who I credit with making me the coach I am today. I will never forget hearing him calling out my name repeatedly to fill the gap at an awards ceremony where I was taking a long time getting to the stage, 'It's Karen Kissane. Karen Kissane, everyone.' His voice still plays over in my mind from this occasion and so many of his classes that I attended. He was a true master of his craft, and I still can't believe he's not here today.

Let's also not forget that the world is a better place because of the coaches who dedicate themselves to transforming lives. You're the unsung heroes, the changemakers, and the champions of personal growth. Keep shining, keep coaching, and keep making the world a brighter place, one remarkable coaching session at a time.

And lastly, to all aspiring authors,

Remember that writing a book is like a never-ending game of hide-and-seek. But when you finally emerge from your creative hiding spot, the joy is immeasurable. Keep chasing your dreams – you never know what remarkable adventures lie ahead.

With heartfelt gratitude and a sigh of relief, Karen.

Your implementation checklist

The Kind of Coach You Really Want to Be

- Your thoughts, beliefs, attitudes, ideas, and the limitations you place on yourself, consciously or subconsciously, determine your type of business and overall success.
- Having the right strategy is only part of the puzzle and this needs to be combined with the confidence to take action and an attitude to succeed no matter what.

Introducing the Signature Framework

- Being a great coach is not the same as having a great coaching business.
- Coaches typically fall into one of three stages of growth: being time-rich but client-poor, being client-rich but time-poor or being client-rich and time-rich.
- The Signature Framework I'm going to share with you will show you how to move from the first two stages into being client-rich and time-rich.

Step #1: Setting Yourself Up for Success

- When you take the time to set yourself up for success, you'll feel more prepared and motivated to work on your business.
  - Action 1: Get in the right mindset
  - Action 2: Adjust your daily habits
  - Action 3: Check where your business is today
  - Action 4: Create a roadmap
  - Action 5: Set your financial targets
  - Action 6: Step into your Queen Bee role

Step #2: Know the Pillars of Your Business

- Knowing the pillars of your business is knowing what you stand for. They will allow you to stand head and shoulders above others in your field and show your future clients that you can help them.
  - Action 1: Define your brand
  - Action 2: Tell people about your business pillars and what your business stands for
  - Action 3: Share your story with authenticity
  - Action 4: Get clear on your messaging

Step #3: Understanding Your Product or Service and the Problem it Solves

- Being able to articulate who you help and, crucially, what you help them achieve, is a must. Clarity on outcomes is often the biggest sticking point most people have in their business; without this it is likely you won't reach the right people, and your message won't be heard.
    - Action 1: Differentiate features from benefits and understand the importance of outcomes
    - Action 2: Know what it takes for people to know, like, and trust your brand
    - Action 3: Craft your mission statement

Step #4: Creating Irresistible Offers

- The most sustainable businesses have a range of revenue streams. Packaging your services into irresistible offers will help you look at new ways to generate revenue that enables you to reach higher income levels.
    - Action 1: Have a signature system for how you help your clients
    - Action 2: Build a product ladder
    - Action 3: Work out your pricing strategies

Step #5: Building Consistent, Predictable Revenue

- If you have big aspirations and crave more freedom, choices and wealth, you'll need a way of generating leads. This means having some sort of sales funnel and lead generation strategy for your business because this is how you generate predictable sales.
    - Action 1: Realise the potential of the online space
    - Action 2: Understand the power of having a sales funnel
    - Action 3: Don't Just Talk to the Dot
    - Action 4: Nail down the elements of a funnel
    - Action 5: Have a plan for each step in your client's buying journey

Step #6: Building More Visibility

- If you want to make repeatable sales in your business, you need a big enough pond to fish in. Building an audience isn't just about finding people to sell your products and services to. You have to also build a relationship with those people by demonstrating your position and credibility as a coach.
  - Action 1: Use fear as fuel to put yourself out there
  - Action 2: Build an audience organically first
  - Action 3: Utilise Facebook groups
  - Action 4: Create a freebie/opt-in/lead magnet
  - Action 5: Master email marketing

STEP #7: CRAFT A WINNING CONTENT STRATEGY

- Our content as a business owner is the currency with which we attract our audience, engage with them, and convert them to paying customers. As a business owner, you should be on social media to take advantage of its visibility.
  - Action 1: Reframe your mindset around social media
  - Action 2: Craft your brand guidelines around a deep understanding of your audience
  - Action 3: Define your content pillars and map out your content calendar
  - Action 4: Grow your social media numbers and boost engagement
  - Action 5: Follow the rules of copywriting for social media

Step #8: Sell Confidently

- You must develop selling skills to have a thriving business. Sales are the beating heart of your business that will secure its longevity and ensure your support for future clients, while providing for you and your family.
  - Action 1: Reframe your mindset around selling
  - Action 2: Craft a sound sales plan
  - Action 3: Know when to upsell and downsell
  - Action 4: Overcome objections with comfort
  - Action 5: Realise the power of storytelling
  - Action 6: Master winning sales calls

Step #9: Implement Systems That Make Your Business Run Like Clockwork

- The first step to creating a business that runs like clockwork is realising you don't have to be the person doing everything within your company. At the core of all productivity are delegation and simplified systems. These allow us to leverage our time and get more done so that we can focus on our zone of excellence, which is coaching our clients and being the show-pony, rather than the work-horse in our business.
  - Action 1: Define your processes
  - Action 2: Automate
  - Action 3: Outsource where necessary
  - Action 4: Embrace AI

Printed in Great Britain
by Amazon